MW00950872

日本料理

Make It Easy Japanese Home Cooking Cookbook for Beginners

2

Table of

Contents

日本料理

DIRECTIONS:

1. In a large pot, heat vegetable oil over medium-high heat. Add pork belly slices and cook until browned on both sides. Remove and set aside.

2. In the same pot, add pork shank bones, onion, garlic, ginger, and green onions. Cook until aromatic, about 5 minutes.

3. Pour in water and bring to a boil. Reduce heat to low and simmer uncovered for 8 hours, skimming off any foam that rises to the surface.

4. Once the broth is rich and flavorful, strain it through a fine-mesh sieve into another pot. Discard solids.

5. Season the broth with soy sauce, sesame oil, and salt to taste.

6. Meanwhile, cook the ramen noodles according to package instructions. Drain and set aside.

7. To serve, divide cooked noodles among serving bowls. Ladle hot broth over the noodles.

8. Arrange pork belly slices, soft-boiled eggs, nori seaweed, and any desired toppings on top of the noodles.

9. Serve hot and enjoy your homemade Tonkotsu Ramen!

Calories	Servings	Prep Time	Cook Time
600	4	15M	8Hs

INGREDIENTS:

- 4 pork shank bones
- 1 pound pork belly, sliced
- 1 onion, halved
- 4 cloves garlic, smashed
- 1 thumb-sized piece of ginger, sliced
- 2 green onions, chopped
- 2 tablespoons vegetable oil
- 8 cups water
- 4 packs of ramen noodles (about 400g)
- 4 soft-boiled eggs, peeled and halved
- 4 sheets nori seaweed
- 4 tablespoons soy sauce
- 2 teaspoons sesame oil
- Salt, to taste
- Optional toppings: sliced green onions, bamboo shoots, corn kernels, narutomaki (fish cake), mushrooms

Calories	Servings	Prep Time	Cook Time
550	4	20M	30M

INGREDIENTS:

- 4 packs of ramen noodles (about 400g)
- 4 cups chicken or vegetable broth
- 4 cups water
- 1/2 cup white miso paste
- 2 tablespoons soy sauce
- 2 tablespoons sesame oil
- 2 tablespoons vegetable oil
- 1 onion, thinly sliced
- 4 cloves garlic, minced
- 1 thumb-sized piece of ginger, grated
- 1 cup sliced mushrooms (shiitake, button, or cremini)
- 2 cups baby spinach leaves
- 4 soft-boiled eggs, peeled and halved
- 2 green onions, thinly sliced
- Optional toppings: cooked chicken or pork slices, bamboo shoots, corn kernels, nori seaweed, sesame seeds

DIRECTIONS:

1. In a large pot, heat vegetable oil over medium heat. Add sliced onions and cook until translucent, about 5 minutes.

2. Add minced garlic and grated ginger to the pot. Cook for another 2 minutes until fragrant.

3. Pour chicken or vegetable broth and water into the pot. Bring to a simmer.

4. In a small bowl, whisk together miso paste, soy sauce, and sesame oil until smooth. Add this miso mixture to the pot, stirring well to combine.

5. Add sliced mushrooms to the broth and simmer for 10 minutes until mushrooms are tender.

6. Meanwhile, cook the ramen noodles according to package instructions. Drain and set aside.

7. To serve, divide cooked noodles among serving bowls. Ladle hot miso broth over the noodles.

8. Add a handful of baby spinach leaves to each bowl.

9. Garnish with soft-boiled eggs, sliced green onions, and any desired toppings.

10. Serve hot and enjoy your homemade Miso Ramen!

DIRECTIONS:

1. In a large pot, heat vegetable oil over medium heat. Add minced garlic and sliced ginger. Cook until fragrant, about 1 minute.

2. Pour in chicken or vegetable broth, water, soy sauce, mirin, sake, and sugar. Bring to a simmer.

3. Simmer for 30 minutes, allowing the flavors to meld.

4. Meanwhile, cook the ramen noodles according to package instructions. Drain and set aside.

5. Strain the broth through a fine-mesh sieve into a separate pot or serving vessel.

6. To serve, divide cooked noodles among serving bowls.

7. Pour the hot broth into individual serving bowls, alongside the noodles.

8. Serve with optional toppings such as sliced pork belly or chicken, soft-boiled eggs, bamboo shoots, nori seaweed, sliced green onions, sesame seeds, and chili oil on the side.

9. To eat, dip the noodles into the broth and enjoy your homemade Tsukemen!

Calories	Servings	Prep Time	Cook Time
580	4	30M	1H

INGREDIENTS:

- 4 packs of ramen noodles (about 400g)
- 4 cups chicken or vegetable broth
- 1 cup water
- 1/4 cup soy sauce
- 2 tablespoons mirin (Japanese sweet rice wine)
- 2 tablespoons sake (or dry white wine)
- 1 tablespoon sugar
- 2 cloves garlic, minced
- 1 thumb-sized piece of ginger, sliced
- 2 green onions, chopped
- 1 tablespoon vegetable oil
- Optional toppings: sliced pork belly or chicken, soft-boiled eggs, bamboo shoots, nori seaweed, sliced green onions, sesame seeds, chili oil

Calories	Servings	Prep Time	Cook Time
580	4	15M	30M

INGREDIENTS:

- 4 packs of ramen noodles (about 400g)
- 4 cups chicken or vegetable broth
- 2 cups water
- 1/4 cup white miso paste
- 4 tablespoons unsalted butter
- 1 cup corn kernels (fresh or frozen)
- 2 cloves garlic, minced
- 1 thumb-sized piece of ginger, grated
- 2 green onions, thinly sliced
- 2 tablespoons soy sauce
- 1 tablespoon sesame oil
- Salt and pepper, to taste
- Optional toppings: soft-boiled eggs, sliced bamboo shoots, nori seaweed, sliced green onions, sesame seeds

DIRECTIONS:

1. In a large pot, combine chicken or vegetable broth and water. Bring to a simmer over medium heat.

2. In a small bowl, mix together miso paste and a ladleful of hot broth until smooth. Pour the miso mixture back into the pot and stir well to combine.

3. In a separate pan, melt unsalted butter over medium heat. Add minced garlic and grated ginger. Cook until fragrant, about 1 minute.

4. Add corn kernels to the pan and sauté for 5-7 minutes until lightly golden brown.

5. Meanwhile, cook the ramen noodles according to package instructions. Drain and set aside.

6. Season the miso broth with soy sauce, sesame oil, salt, and pepper to taste.

7. To serve, divide cooked noodles among serving bowls.

8. Ladle hot miso broth over the noodles.

9. Top each bowl with sautéed corn, sliced green onions, and any optional toppings you desire.

10. Enjoy your homemade Miso Butter Corn Ramen!

Directions:

1. Cook the ramen noodles according to package instructions. Drain and set aside.

2. In a large skillet or wok, heat vegetable oil over medium-high heat. Add sliced pork belly or bacon and cook until browned and crispy.

3. Add minced garlic and grated ginger to the skillet. Cook for another 2 minutes until fragrant.

4. Stir in soy sauce, mirin, and sesame oil. Cook for an additional 1-2 minutes to coat the meat evenly.

5. Add cooked ramen noodles to the skillet. Toss well to combine and coat the noodles with the sauce.

6. Divide the seasoned noodles among serving bowls.

7. Top each bowl with soft-boiled eggs, sliced green onions, cooked corn kernels, bamboo shoots, and shredded nori seaweed.

8. Optionally, garnish with sesame seeds, a drizzle of chili oil, or grated Parmesan cheese.

9. Serve hot and enjoy your homemade Mazemen (Brothless Ramen)!

Calories	Servings	Prep Time	Cook Time
580	4	15M	20M

Ingredients:

- 4 packs of ramen noodles (about 400g)
- 1/2 pound pork belly or bacon, sliced
- 2 cloves garlic, minced
- 1 thumb-sized piece of ginger, grated
- 2 tablespoons soy sauce
- 2 tablespoons mirin (Japanese sweet rice wine)
- 2 tablespoons sesame oil
- 1 tablespoon vegetable oil
- 4 soft-boiled eggs, peeled and halved
- 2 green onions, thinly sliced
- 1/2 cup corn kernels (fresh or frozen), cooked
- 1/4 cup bamboo shoots, sliced
- 1/4 cup nori seaweed, shredded
  - Optional toppings: sesame seeds, chili oil, grated Parmesan cheese

Calories	Servings	Prep Time	Cook Time
620	4	15M	15M

INGREDIENTS:

- 4 packs of ramen noodles (about 400g)
- 1/2 pound pork belly or bacon, thinly sliced
- 2 cloves garlic, minced
- 1 thumb-sized piece of ginger, grated
- 2 tablespoons vegetable oil
- 1/4 cup soy sauce
- 2 tablespoons mirin (Japanese sweet rice wine)
- 2 tablespoons sake (or dry white wine)
- 1 tablespoon sesame oil
- 2 teaspoons sugar
- 1 teaspoon chili oil (optional)
- 2 green onions, thinly sliced
- 1/4 cup roasted peanuts, chopped (optional)
- 4 soft-boiled eggs, peeled and halved
- Optional toppings: nori seaweed, shredded cabbage, bean sprouts, grated garlic, chili flakes

DIRECTIONS:

1. Cook the ramen noodles according to package instructions. Drain, rinse under cold water, and set aside.

2. In a large skillet or wok, heat vegetable oil over medium-high heat. Add sliced pork belly or bacon and cook until browned and crispy.

3. Add minced garlic and grated ginger to the skillet. Cook for another 2 minutes until fragrant.

4. In a small bowl, mix together soy sauce, mirin, sake, sesame oil, sugar, and chili oil (if using).

5. Pour the sauce mixture into the skillet with the pork belly or bacon. Cook for a few minutes until the sauce thickens slightly.

6. Add the cooked ramen noodles to the skillet. Toss well to coat the noodles evenly with the sauce.

7. Divide the seasoned noodles among serving bowls.

8. Top each bowl with sliced green onions, chopped roasted peanuts (if using), and soft-boiled eggs.

9. Optionally, add additional toppings such as nori seaweed, shredded cabbage, bean sprouts, grated garlic, or chili flakes according to taste.

10. Serve hot and enjoy your homemade Abura Soba (Oily Ramen)!

Miso Soup

DIRECTIONS:

1. In a medium pot, heat vegetable oil over medium heat. Add the pumpkin cubes and sauté for about 5 minutes until they start to soften.

2. Pour in the dashi stock (or vegetable broth) and bring to a simmer. Cook the pumpkin until tender, about 10-15 minutes.

3. In a small bowl, mix the miso paste with a ladleful of the hot broth until smooth.

4. Add the miso mixture back into the pot and stir well to combine.

5. Add soy sauce and mirin to the soup and let it simmer gently for another 5 minutes.

6. Taste and adjust seasoning if necessary.

7. To serve, ladle the Pumpkin Miso Soup into individual bowls and garnish with sliced green onions. Optionally, add tofu cubes, seaweed strips, or sesame seeds for extra flavor and texture.

8. Enjoy this comforting and nutritious Japanese soup as a starter or as part of a meal.

Calories	Servings	Prep Time	Cook Time
90	4	10M	20M

INGREDIENTS:

- 4 cups dashi stock (or vegetable broth for a vegetarian option)
- 1 cup pumpkin or butternut squash, peeled and cubed
- 2 tablespoons miso paste (white or red miso)
- 2 green onions, thinly sliced
- 1 tablespoon soy sauce
- 1 tablespoon mirin (Japanese sweet rice wine)
- 1 tablespoon vegetable oil
- Optional: tofu cubes, seaweed strips (such as nori), sesame seeds for garnish

Calories	Servings	Prep Time	Cook Time
180	4	10M	20M

INGREDIENTS:

- 4 cups dashi stock (or vegetable stock for a vegetarian option)
- 1 cup corn kernels (fresh, frozen, or canned)
- 4 slices bacon, chopped
- 2 tablespoons miso paste (white or red miso)
- 2 green onions, thinly sliced
- 1 tablespoon soy sauce
- 1 tablespoon mirin (Japanese sweet rice wine)
- 1 tablespoon vegetable oil
- Optional: tofu cubes, sliced mushrooms, seaweed strips (such as nori)

DIRECTIONS:

1. Heat vegetable oil in a medium pot over medium heat. Add the chopped bacon and cook until it starts to brown and crisp up, about 5 minutes.

2. Add the corn kernels to the pot and sauté with the bacon for another 2-3 minutes.

3. Pour in the dashi stock (or vegetable stock) and bring to a simmer. Let it cook for about 10 minutes to allow the flavors to meld together.

4. In a small bowl, mix the miso paste with a ladleful of the hot broth until smooth.

5. Add the miso mixture back into the pot and stir well to combine.

6. Add soy sauce and mirin to the soup and let it simmer gently for another 5 minutes.

7. Taste and adjust seasoning if necessary.

8. To serve, ladle the Corn and Bacon Miso Soup into individual bowls and garnish with sliced green onions. Optionally, add tofu cubes, sliced mushrooms, or seaweed strips for extra flavor and texture.

9. Enjoy this comforting and savory Japanese soup as a delightful meal or appetizer.

DIRECTIONS:

1. Heat vegetable oil in a medium pot over medium heat. Add diced tomatoes and cook for 5 minutes until softened.

2. Pour in the vegetable or chicken broth and bring to a simmer.

3. In a small bowl, mix the miso paste with a ladleful of the hot broth until smooth.

4. Add the miso mixture back into the pot and stir well to combine.

5. Add soy sauce, mirin, and chili flakes to the soup and let it simmer gently for another 10 minutes.

6. Taste and adjust seasoning if necessary.

7. If desired, add tofu cubes, sliced mushrooms, spinach, or seaweed strips to the soup and let them cook for a few minutes until tender.

8. To serve, ladle the Spicy Tomato Miso Soup into individual bowls and garnish with sliced green onions.

9. Enjoy this flavorful and slightly spicy twist on traditional miso soup, perfect for warming up on chilly days.

Calories	Servings	Prep Time	Cook Time
130	4	10M	20M

INGREDIENTS:

- 4 cups vegetable or chicken broth
- 1 can (14 oz) diced tomatoes
- 4 tablespoons miso paste (white or red miso)
- 2 green onions, thinly sliced
- 1 tablespoon soy sauce
- 1 tablespoon mirin (Japanese sweet rice wine)
- 1 tablespoon vegetable oil
- 1 teaspoon chili flakes (adjust to taste)
- Optional: tofu cubes, sliced mushrooms, spinach, seaweed strips (such as nori)

Calories	Servings	Prep Time	Cook Time
150	4	15M	25M

INGREDIENTS:

- 4 cups chicken broth
- 3 tablespoons miso paste (white or red)
- 1 boneless, skinless chicken breast, thinly sliced
- 1 carrot, peeled and sliced
- 1 parsnip, peeled and sliced
- 1 small turnip, peeled and diced
- 4 shiitake mushrooms, sliced
- 2 green onions, thinly sliced
- 1 tablespoon soy sauce
- 1 tablespoon mirin (optional)
- 1 tablespoon sesame oil
- 1 tablespoon chopped fresh parsley or cilantro (optional)
- Cooked rice, for serving (optional)

DIRECTIONS:

1. In a pot, bring the chicken broth to a simmer over medium heat.

2. In a small bowl, mix the miso paste with a few tablespoons of the hot chicken broth to dissolve it.

3. Add the dissolved miso paste back into the pot and stir well to combine.

4. Add the sliced chicken breast, carrot, parsnip, turnip, and shiitake mushrooms to the pot.

5. Simmer for about 15-20 minutes, or until the chicken is cooked through and the vegetables are tender.

6. Add sliced green onions, soy sauce, and mirin (if using) to the soup. Stir gently.

7. Taste the soup and adjust seasoning if needed.

8. Just before serving, drizzle sesame oil over the soup.

9. Optionally, garnish with chopped parsley or cilantro for freshness.

10. Serve hot with cooked rice on the side if desired.

11. Enjoy your hearty Chicken and Root Vegetable Miso Soup!

DIRECTIONS:

Calories	Servings	Prep Time	Cook Time
90	4	10M	15M

1. In a pot, bring the vegetable broth or dashi to a simmer over medium heat.

2. In a small bowl, mix the miso paste with a few tablespoons of the hot broth to dissolve it.

3. Add the dissolved miso paste back into the pot and stir well to combine.

4. Add the spinach to the pot and simmer for about 5 minutes, or until wilted.

5. Meanwhile, toast the sesame seeds in a dry skillet over medium heat until lightly golden and fragrant, about 2-3 minutes. Remove from heat and set aside.

6. Add the tofu cubes and sliced green onions to the pot.

7. Simmer for another 5 minutes.

8. Add soy sauce and mirin (if using) to the soup. Stir gently.

9. Taste the soup and adjust seasoning if needed.

10. Just before serving, drizzle sesame oil over the soup and sprinkle with toasted sesame seeds.

11. Serve hot with cooked rice on the side if desired.

12. Enjoy your nutritious Spinach and Sesame Miso Soup!

INGREDIENTS:

- 4 cups vegetable broth or dashi
- 3 tablespoons miso paste (white or red)
- 6 ounces fresh spinach, washed and trimmed
- 2 tablespoons sesame seeds
- 8 ounces silken tofu, cut into small cubes
- 2 green onions, thinly sliced
- 1 tablespoon soy sauce
- 1 tablespoon mirin (optional)
- 1 tablespoon sesame oil
- Cooked rice, for serving (optional)

Calories	Servings	Prep Time	Cook Time
120	4	10M	20M

Ingredients:

- 4 cups vegetable broth or dashi
- 3 tablespoons miso paste (white or red)
- 1 large sweet potato, peeled and diced
- 1 leek, sliced (white and light green parts only)
- 2 tablespoons chopped fresh parsley or cilantro
- 8 ounces firm tofu, cut into small cubes
- 2 green onions, thinly sliced
- 1 tablespoon soy sauce
- 1 tablespoon mirin (optional)
- 1 tablespoon vegetable oil

Directions:

1. In a pot, heat the vegetable oil over medium heat.
2. Add the diced sweet potato and sliced leek. Sauté for about 5 minutes until they start to soften.
3. Pour in the vegetable broth or dashi and bring to a simmer.
4. In a small bowl, mix the miso paste with a few tablespoons of the hot broth to dissolve it.
5. Add the dissolved miso paste back into the pot and stir well to combine.
6. Add the tofu cubes and sliced green onions to the pot.
7. Simmer for about 10-15 minutes, or until the sweet potatoes are tender.
8. Add soy sauce and mirin (if using) to the soup. Stir gently.
9. Taste the soup and adjust seasoning if needed.
10. Just before serving, sprinkle chopped parsley or cilantro over the soup.
11. Serve hot and enjoy your delicious Sweet Potato and Leek Miso Soup!

SUSHI ROLLS

DIRECTIONS:

1. Cook sushi rice according to package instructions. Once cooked, let it cool slightly.

2. In a small bowl, mix together mayonnaise, Sriracha sauce (if using), rice vinegar, and sugar.

3. Lay a nori seaweed sheet on a bamboo sushi mat or a clean kitchen towel. Moisten your hands with water and spread about 1/2 cup of cooked sushi rice evenly over the nori, leaving a 1-inch border at the top.

4. Place tuna slices and avocado slices in the center of the rice.

5. Drizzle some of the mayo mixture over the filling.

6. Carefully roll the sushi using the bamboo mat or towel, pressing gently to shape it into a tight cylinder. Seal the edge with a bit of water.

7. Repeat the process with the remaining nori sheets and ingredients.

8. Slice each roll into 8 pieces using a sharp knife, wiping the knife clean between cuts.

9. Serve the tuna avocado rolls with soy sauce, pickled ginger, and wasabi on the side. Enjoy your homemade Japanese delicacy!

Calories	Servings	Prep Time	Cook Time
280	4	25M	10M

INGREDIENTS:

- 2 cups sushi rice
- 4 nori seaweed sheets
- 1/2 pound sushi-grade tuna, thinly sliced
- 1 ripe avocado, peeled, pitted, and sliced
- 1 tablespoon mayonnaise
- 1 teaspoon Sriracha sauce (optional)
- 1 teaspoon rice vinegar
- 1/2 teaspoon sugar
- Soy sauce, for serving
- Pickled ginger, for serving
- Wasabi, for serving

Calories	Servings	Prep Time	Cook Time
340	4	30M	20M

INGREDIENTS:

- 2 cups sushi rice
- 4 nori seaweed sheets
- 12 large shrimp, peeled and deveined
- 1 cup tempura batter mix
- Vegetable oil, for frying
- 1 avocado, peeled, pitted, and sliced
- 1/4 cup mayonnaise
- 2 tablespoons Sriracha sauce
- 1 tablespoon rice vinegar
- 1/2 teaspoon sugar
- Soy sauce, for serving
- Pickled ginger, for serving
- Wasabi, for serving

DIRECTIONS:

1. Cook sushi rice according to package instructions. Once cooked, let it cool slightly.

2. Prepare tempura batter according to package instructions.

3. Heat vegetable oil in a deep pan or fryer to 350°F (180°C).

4. Dip shrimp into the tempura batter, ensuring they are evenly coated, then carefully place them into the hot oil. Fry until golden brown and crispy, about 2-3 minutes. Remove and drain on paper towels.

5. In a small bowl, mix together mayonnaise, Sriracha sauce, rice vinegar, and sugar to make the spicy mayo sauce.

6. Lay a nori seaweed sheet on a bamboo sushi mat or a clean kitchen towel. Moisten your hands with water and spread about 1/2 cup of cooked sushi rice evenly over the nori, leaving a 1-inch border at the top.

7. Arrange avocado slices and tempura shrimp in the center of the rice.

8. Drizzle some spicy mayo sauce over the filling.

9. Carefully roll the sushi using the bamboo mat or towel, pressing gently to shape it into a tight cylinder. Seal the edge with a bit of water.

10. Repeat the process with the remaining nori sheets and ingredients.

11. Slice each roll into 8 pieces using a sharp knife, wiping the knife clean between cuts.

12. Serve the shrimp tempura rolls with soy sauce, pickled ginger, and wasabi on the side. Enjoy your homemade Japanese delight!

SUSHI ROLLS

DIRECTIONS:

1. Cook sushi rice according to package instructions. Once cooked, let it cool slightly.

2. In a small bowl, mix together mayonnaise, Sriracha sauce, rice vinegar, and sugar to create the dynamite sauce.

3. Combine the shredded imitation crab meat with the dynamite sauce until well coated.

4. Lay a nori seaweed sheet on a bamboo sushi mat or a clean kitchen towel. Moisten your hands with water and spread about 1/2 cup of cooked sushi rice evenly over the nori, leaving a 1-inch border at the top.

5. Spread a layer of the crab dynamite mixture across the center of the rice.

6. Place avocado slices on top of the crab mixture.

7. Carefully roll the sushi using the bamboo mat or towel, pressing gently to shape it into a tight cylinder. Seal the edge with a bit of water.

8. Repeat the process with the remaining nori sheets and ingredients.

9. Slice each roll into 8 pieces using a sharp knife, wiping the knife clean between cuts.

10. Serve the crab dynamite rolls with soy sauce, pickled ginger, and wasabi on the side. Optionally, garnish with sesame seeds and thinly sliced green onions. Enjoy your homemade Japanese delight!

Calories	Servings	Prep Time	Cook Time
290	4	20M	10M

INGREDIENTS:

- 2 cups sushi rice
- 4 nori seaweed sheets
- 1/2 pound imitation crab meat, shredded
- 1/4 cup mayonnaise
- 1 tablespoon Sriracha sauce
- 1 teaspoon rice vinegar
- 1/2 teaspoon sugar
- 1 avocado, peeled, pitted, and sliced
- Soy sauce, for serving
- Pickled ginger, for serving
- Wasabi, for serving
- Sesame seeds, for garnish (optional)
- Green onions, thinly sliced, for garnish (optional)

Calories	Servings	Prep Time	Cook Time
300	4	25M	10M

INGREDIENTS:

- 2 cups sushi rice
- 4 nori seaweed sheets
- 1/2 pound yellowtail fish fillet, thinly sliced
- 1/4 cup mayonnaise
- 2 tablespoons Sriracha sauce
- 1 tablespoon rice vinegar
- 1/2 teaspoon sugar
- Soy sauce, for serving
- Pickled ginger, for serving
- Wasabi, for serving
- Sesame seeds, for garnish (optional)
- Thinly sliced cucumber, for garnish (optional)

DIRECTIONS:

1. Cook sushi rice according to package instructions. Once cooked, let it cool slightly.

2. In a small bowl, mix together mayonnaise, Sriracha sauce, rice vinegar, and sugar to make the spicy mayo sauce.

3. Lay a nori seaweed sheet on a bamboo sushi mat or a clean kitchen towel. Moisten your hands with water and spread about 1/2 cup of cooked sushi rice evenly over the nori, leaving a 1-inch border at the top.

4. Place yellowtail slices in the center of the rice.

5. Drizzle some spicy mayo sauce over the yellowtail.

6. Carefully roll the sushi using the bamboo mat or towel, pressing gently to shape it into a tight cylinder. Seal the edge with a bit of water.

7. Repeat the process with the remaining nori sheets and ingredients.

8. Slice each roll into 8 pieces using a sharp knife, wiping the knife clean between cuts.

9. Serve the spicy yellowtail rolls with soy sauce, pickled ginger, and wasabi on the side. Optionally, garnish with sesame seeds and thinly sliced cucumber. Enjoy your homemade Japanese delight!

DIRECTIONS:

Calories	Servings	Prep Time	Cook Time
150	4	15M	0M

1. Cook sushi rice according to package instructions and let it cool to room temperature.

2. Place a sheet of nori shiny side down on a bamboo sushi rolling mat.

3. Spread a thin layer of sushi rice evenly over the nori, leaving about half an inch of space at the top edge.

4. Arrange julienned cucumber strips horizontally across the center of the rice.

5. Starting from the bottom edge, tightly roll the sushi using the bamboo mat, applying gentle pressure to shape it into a cylinder.

6. Seal the edge of the nori with a bit of water to secure the roll.

7. Repeat the process with the remaining ingredients to make three more rolls.

8. Use a sharp knife to slice each roll into 6-8 pieces.

9. Serve the Cucumber Rolls with soy sauce, wasabi, and pickled ginger on the side.

10. Enjoy your homemade sushi rolls as a refreshing and light snack or appetizer.</li>

INGREDIENTS:

- 4 sheets nori (seaweed)
- 2 cups sushi rice
- 1 large cucumber, julienned
- Soy sauce, for dipping
- Wasabi, for serving
- Pickled ginger, for serving

Calories	Servings	Prep Time	Cook Time
160	4	15M	0M

INGREDIENTS:

- 1/2 pound sushi-grade salmon fillet
- 2 tablespoons extra virgin olive oil
- 1 tablespoon lemon juice
- 1 teaspoon soy sauce
- 1 teaspoon honey
- Salt and black pepper, to taste
- 1 tablespoon chopped fresh dill, for garnish
- 1 tablespoon capers, drained and rinsed, for garnish
- Optional: microgreens, thinly sliced radishes, shaved Parmesan cheese

DIRECTIONS:

1. Place the salmon fillet on a clean cutting board and use a sharp knife to slice it thinly against the grain.

2. Arrange the sliced salmon on a serving plate, slightly overlapping.

3. In a small bowl, whisk together extra virgin olive oil, lemon juice, soy sauce, and honey to make the dressing.

4. Drizzle the dressing over the sliced salmon.

5. Season the salmon carpaccio with salt and black pepper to taste.

6. Sprinkle chopped fresh dill and capers over the salmon slices for garnish.

7. Optionally, garnish with microgreens, thinly sliced radishes, or shaved Parmesan cheese.

8. Serve immediately as an appetizer or light meal.

9. Enjoy your homemade Salmon Carpaccio!

DIRECTIONS:

1. Slice the sushi-grade tuna loin thinly against the grain and arrange the slices on a serving plate.

2. In a small bowl, whisk together soy sauce, mirin, rice vinegar, sesame oil, grated ginger, grated garlic, and sugar to make the marinade.

3. Pour the marinade over the sliced tuna, ensuring that all pieces are well coated. Let it marinate for about 5-10 minutes.

4. Optionally, garnish the marinated tuna with sliced green onions, sesame seeds, and red pepper flakes for added flavor and presentation.

5. Serve immediately as an appetizer or part of a sushi platter.

6. Enjoy your homemade Maguro Zuke (Marinated Tuna)!

Calories	Servings	Prep Time	Cook Time
200	4	10M	0M

INGREDIENTS:

- 1/2 pound sushi-grade tuna loin
- 1/4 cup soy sauce
- 2 tablespoons mirin (Japanese sweet rice wine)
- 1 tablespoon rice vinegar
- 1 tablespoon sesame oil
- 1 teaspoon grated ginger
- 1 teaspoon grated garlic
- 1 teaspoon sugar
- Optional: sliced green onions, sesame seeds, red pepper flakes

HIRAME (HALIBUT)
SASHIMI

Calories	Servings	Prep Time	Cook Time
180	4	10M	0M

INGREDIENTS:

- 1/2 pound sushi-grade halibut fillet (hirame)
- Soy sauce, for dipping
- Wasabi paste, for serving
- Pickled ginger, for serving
- Optional: thinly sliced radishes, microgreens, lemon wedges

DIRECTIONS:

1. Slice the sushi-grade halibut fillet into thin slices against the grain.

2. Arrange the slices on a serving plate.

3. Serve with soy sauce and wasabi paste on the side for dipping.

4. Optionally, serve with pickled ginger, thinly sliced radishes, microgreens, or lemon wedges for added flavor and presentation.

5. Serve immediately as an appetizer or part of a sushi platter.

6. Enjoy your homemade Hirame (Halibut) sashimi!

DIRECTIONS:

Calories	Servings	Prep Time	Cook Time
120	4	5M	0M

1. Carefully rinse the salmon roe under cold water to remove any excess salt or debris.

2. Gently pat the salmon roe dry with paper towels.

3. Arrange the salmon roe on a serving plate.

4. Drizzle with soy sauce, if desired.

5. Optionally, serve with thinly sliced nori seaweed and steamed rice.

6. Serve immediately as an appetizer or part of a sushi platter.

7. Enjoy your homemade Ikura (Salmon Roe) sashimi!

INGREDIENTS:

- 1/2 pound salmon roe (ikura)
- Soy sauce, for drizzling
- Optional: thinly sliced nori seaweed, steamed rice

Calories	Servings	Prep Time	Cook Time
160	4	10M	0M

INGREDIENTS:

- 1/2 pound sushi-grade red snapper fillet (tai)
- Soy sauce, for dipping
- Wasabi paste, for serving
- Pickled ginger, for serving
- Optional: thinly sliced radishes, microgreens, lemon wedges

DIRECTIONS:

1. Slice the sushi-grade red snapper fillet thinly against the grain.

2. Arrange the slices on a serving plate.

3. Serve with soy sauce and wasabi paste on the side for dipping.

4. Optionally, serve with pickled ginger, thinly sliced radishes, microgreens, or lemon wedges for added flavor and presentation.

5. Serve immediately as an appetizer or part of a sushi platter.

6. Enjoy your homemade Tai (Red Snapper) sashimi!

DIRECTIONS:

1. Rinse the shishito peppers and pat them dry with paper towels.

2. Heat vegetable oil in a deep fryer or large pot to 350°F (180°C).

3. In a mixing bowl, combine all-purpose flour and ice-cold water. Mix lightly; it's okay if the batter is slightly lumpy.

4. Dip each shishito pepper into the tempura batter until well coated.

5. Carefully lower the coated shishito peppers into the hot oil and fry for about 2-3 minutes until golden brown and crispy.

6. Use a slotted spoon to remove the tempura from the oil and drain on paper towels.

7. Sprinkle the fried shishito peppers with salt while they are still hot.

8. Serve immediately with tempura dipping sauce on the side.

9. Enjoy your homemade Shishito Pepper Tempura!

Calories	Servings	Prep Time	Cook Time
150	4	10M	10M

INGREDIENTS:

- 1/2 pound shishito peppers
- 1 cup all-purpose flour
- 1 cup ice-cold water
- Vegetable oil, for frying
- Salt, to taste
- Tempura dipping sauce (store-bought or homemade), for serving

Calories	Servings	Prep Time	Cook Time
220	4	15M	10M

INGREDIENTS:

- 1 lotus root, peeled and thinly sliced
- 1 cup all-purpose flour
- 1 cup ice-cold water
- Vegetable oil, for frying
- Salt, to taste
- Tempura dipping sauce (store-bought or homemade), for serving

DIRECTIONS:

1. Rinse the lotus root slices under cold water and pat them dry with paper towels.

2. Heat vegetable oil in a deep fryer or large pot to 350°F (180°C).

3. In a mixing bowl, combine all-purpose flour and ice-cold water. Mix lightly; it's okay if the batter is slightly lumpy.

4. Dip each lotus root slice into the tempura batter until well coated.

5. Carefully lower the coated lotus root slices into the hot oil and fry for about 2-3 minutes until golden brown and crispy.

6. Use a slotted spoon to remove the tempura from the oil and drain on paper towels.

7. Sprinkle the fried lotus root slices with salt while they are still hot.

8. Serve immediately with tempura dipping sauce on the side.

9. Enjoy your homemade Lotus Root Tempura!

DIRECTIONS:

1. Pat the sea eel pieces dry with paper towels.

2. Heat vegetable oil in a deep fryer or large pot to 350°F (180°C).

3. In a mixing bowl, combine all-purpose flour and ice-cold water. Mix lightly; it's okay if the batter is slightly lumpy.

4. Dip each sea eel piece into the tempura batter until well coated.

5. Carefully lower the coated sea eel pieces into the hot oil and fry for about 2-3 minutes until golden brown and crispy.

6. Use a slotted spoon to remove the tempura from the oil and drain on paper towels.

7. Sprinkle the fried sea eel tempura with salt while they are still hot.

8. Serve immediately with tempura dipping sauce on the side.

9. Enjoy your homemade Anago (Sea Eel) Tempura!

Calories	Servings	Prep Time	Cook Time
280	4	20M	10M

INGREDIENTS:

- 4 pieces of sea eel (anago), boneless
- 1 cup all-purpose flour
- 1 cup ice-cold water
- Vegetable oil, for frying
- Salt, to taste
- Tempura dipping sauce (store-bought or homemade), for serving

Calories	Servings	Prep Time	Cook Time
180	4	20M	10M

INGREDIENTS:

- 1/2 small kabocha squash (about 1 pound)
- 1 cup all-purpose flour
- 1 cup ice-cold water
- Vegetable oil, for frying
- Salt, to taste
- Tempura dipping sauce (store-bought or homemade), for serving

DIRECTIONS:

1. Cut the kabocha squash into thin slices, about 1/4 inch thick. Remove the seeds and peel if desired.

2. Heat vegetable oil in a deep fryer or large pot to 350°F (180°C).

3. In a mixing bowl, combine all-purpose flour and ice-cold water. Mix lightly; it's okay if the batter is slightly lumpy.

4. Dip each kabocha slice into the tempura batter until well coated.

5. Carefully lower the coated kabocha slices into the hot oil and fry for about 2-3 minutes until golden brown and crispy.

6. Use a slotted spoon to remove the tempura from the oil and drain on paper towels.

7. Sprinkle the fried kabocha tempura with salt while they are still hot.

8. Serve immediately with tempura dipping sauce on the side.

9. Enjoy your homemade Kabocha (Pumpkin) Tempura!

DIRECTIONS:

1. Heat vegetable oil in a deep fryer or large pot to 350°F (180°C).

2. In a mixing bowl, combine all-purpose flour and ice-cold water. Mix lightly; it's okay if the batter is slightly lumpy.

3. Dip each squid leg into the tempura batter until well coated.

4. Carefully lower the coated squid legs into the hot oil and fry for about 2-3 minutes until golden brown and crispy.

5. Use a slotted spoon to remove the tempura from the oil and drain on paper towels.

6. Sprinkle the fried squid legs tempura with salt while they are still hot.

7. Serve immediately with tempura dipping sauce on the side.

8. Enjoy your homemade Geso (Squid Legs) Tempura!

Calories	Servings	Prep Time	Cook Time
220	4	15M	10M

INGREDIENTS:

- 1 pound squid legs (geso), cleaned and patted dry
- 1 cup all-purpose flour
- 1 cup ice-cold water
- Vegetable oil, for frying
- Salt, to taste
- Tempura dipping sauce (store-bought or homemade), for serving

TEKKADON (TUNA BOWL)

DONBURI

Calories	Servings	Prep Time	Cook Time
400	4	15M	0M

INGREDIENTS:

- 2 cups cooked Japanese rice
- 2 cans (5 ounces each) tuna in water, drained
- 2 tablespoons soy sauce
- 1 tablespoon sesame oil
- 1 tablespoon rice vinegar
- 1 teaspoon sugar
- 1/2 teaspoon grated ginger
- 1/2 teaspoon grated garlic
- 1/4 teaspoon red pepper flakes (optional)
- 2 green onions, thinly sliced
- 1 avocado, sliced
- 1 cucumber, thinly sliced
- Nori strips, for garnish
- Toasted sesame seeds, for garnish

DIRECTIONS:

1. In a small bowl, combine soy sauce, sesame oil, rice vinegar, sugar, grated ginger, grated garlic, and red pepper flakes (if using). Mix well to make the marinade.

2. Place drained tuna in a separate bowl and pour the marinade over it. Toss gently to coat the tuna evenly. Let it marinate for about 10 minutes.

3. Divide cooked rice among serving bowls.

4. Top each bowl of rice with marinated tuna, sliced avocado, and cucumber.

5. Garnish with sliced green onions, nori strips, and toasted sesame seeds.

6. Serve immediately.

7. Enjoy your homemade Tekkadon (Tuna Bowl)!

DONBURI

DIRECTIONS:

1. In a small bowl, whisk together soy sauce, rice vinegar, sesame oil, and sugar to make the dressing.

2. Divide cooked rice among serving bowls.

3. Arrange sliced or cubed seafood, avocado, cucumber, imitation crab meat, and radishes on top of the rice.

4. Drizzle the dressing over the seafood and vegetables.

5. Garnish with pickled ginger, nori strips, toasted sesame seeds, and sliced green onions.

6. Serve immediately.

7. Enjoy your homemade Kaisendon (Seafood Bowl)!

Calories	Servings	Prep Time	Cook Time
450	4	20M	0M

INGREDIENTS:

- 2 cups cooked Japanese rice
- 8 ounces sashimi-grade seafood (such as tuna, salmon, yellowtail, shrimp, or squid), thinly sliced or cubed
- 1 avocado, sliced
- 1 cucumber, thinly sliced
- 1/2 cup imitation crab meat, shredded
- 4 radishes, thinly sliced
- 1/4 cup pickled ginger
- 2 tablespoons soy sauce
- 1 tablespoon rice vinegar
- 1 tablespoon sesame oil
- 1 teaspoon sugar
- Nori strips, for garnish
- Toasted sesame seeds, for garnish
- Sliced green onions, for garnish

UNAJIDON (EEL BOWL)
DONBURI

Calories	Servings	Prep Time	Cook Time
560	4	20M	30M

INGREDIENTS:

- 2 cups cooked Japanese rice
- 2 unagi (eel) fillets, cooked and deboned
- 1/4 cup soy sauce
- 2 tablespoons mirin (Japanese sweet rice wine)
- 1 tablespoon sake (or dry sherry)
- 2 tablespoons sugar
- 1 tablespoon vegetable oil
- 1 onion, thinly sliced
- 4 eggs
- Toasted sesame seeds, for garnish
- Pickled ginger, for serving (optional)
- Nori strips, for garnish (optional)

DIRECTIONS:

1. Preheat the oven to 375°F (190°C).

2. In a small saucepan, combine soy sauce, mirin, sake, and sugar. Heat over medium heat until the sugar dissolves and the mixture slightly thickens, about 5 minutes.

3. Place the unagi fillets on a baking sheet lined with aluminum foil. Brush the fillets with the sauce mixture.

4. Bake in the preheated oven for 15-20 minutes, or until the eel is heated through and slightly caramelized.

5. While the eel is baking, heat vegetable oil in a skillet over medium heat. Add sliced onions and cook until softened and caramelized, about 10-15 minutes. Set aside.

6. In a separate pan, fry the eggs sunny-side-up or over-easy.

7. To assemble, divide the cooked rice among serving bowls. Place the caramelized onions on top of the rice.

8. Place a portion of the cooked unagi fillet on each bowl.

9. Top each bowl with a fried egg.

10. Garnish with toasted sesame seeds and nori strips, if desired.

11. Serve hot with pickled ginger on the side, if desired.

12. Enjoy your homemade Unajidon (Eel Bowl)!

DIRECTIONS:

1. In a mixing bowl, combine ground meat, chopped onion, minced garlic, soy sauce, Worcestershire sauce, salt, and pepper. Mix until well combined.

2. Divide the meat mixture into equal portions and shape them into oval patties.

3. Set up a breading station with three shallow bowls: one with all-purpose flour, one with beaten eggs, and one with panko breadcrumbs.

4. Dredge each meat patty in flour, then dip it into the beaten eggs, and finally coat it evenly with panko breadcrumbs.

5. Heat vegetable oil in a large skillet over medium heat. Fry the breaded meat patties until golden brown and cooked through, about 4-5 minutes per side. Transfer to a plate lined with paper towels to drain excess oil.

6. In the same skillet, pour in tonkatsu sauce and heat it until warm.

7. To assemble, divide the cooked rice among serving bowls. Place a portion of shredded cabbage on top of the rice.

8. Top with the fried minced meat cutlets.

9. Drizzle tonkatsu sauce over the cutlets.

10. Garnish with sliced green onions and toasted sesame seeds.

11. Serve hot.

12. Enjoy your homemade Menchi Katsu Don (Minced Meat Cutlet Bowl)!

Calories	Servings	Prep Time	Cook Time
480	4	20M	20M

INGREDIENTS:

- 2 cups cooked Japanese rice
- 1 pound ground beef or pork
- 1 small onion, finely chopped
- 1 clove garlic, minced
- 1 tablespoon soy sauce
- 1 tablespoon Worcestershire sauce
- Salt and pepper, to taste
- 1/2 cup all-purpose flour
- 2 eggs, beaten
- 1 cup panko breadcrumbs
- Vegetable oil, for frying
- Tonkatsu sauce, for serving
- Finely shredded cabbage, for serving
- Sliced green onions, for garnish
- Toasted sesame seeds, for garnish

Calories	Servings	Prep Time	Cook Time
380	4	15M	30M

INGREDIENTS:

- 1 pound pork belly, sliced
- 1/4 cup soy sauce
- 2 tablespoons mirin (Japanese sweet rice wine)
- 2 tablespoons sake (or dry sherry)
- 2 tablespoons brown sugar
- 2 cloves garlic, minced
- 1 teaspoon grated ginger
- 1 tablespoon vegetable oil
- 2 green onions, thinly sliced, for garnish
- Cooked rice, for serving
- Steamed vegetables, for serving (optional)

DIRECTIONS:

1. In a bowl, mix together soy sauce, mirin, sake, brown sugar, minced garlic, and grated ginger to make the teriyaki sauce.

2. Heat vegetable oil in a skillet over medium heat. Add the pork belly slices and cook until browned on both sides.

3. Pour the teriyaki sauce over the pork belly slices in the skillet.

4. Reduce heat to low and simmer, uncovered, for about 20-25 minutes, or until the sauce has thickened and the pork belly is cooked through, flipping the slices occasionally.

5. Once the pork belly is cooked and the sauce has thickened, remove from heat.

6. Serve the teriyaki pork belly over cooked rice.

7. Garnish with sliced green onions.

8. Serve hot with steamed vegetables on the side, if desired.

9. Enjoy your homemade Teriyaki Pork Belly!

DIRECTIONS:

1. Preheat the oven to 400°F (200°C).

2. In a bowl, mix together soy sauce, mirin, sake, brown sugar, minced garlic, and grated ginger to make the teriyaki sauce.

3. Place the chicken wings in a large mixing bowl and pour half of the teriyaki sauce over them. Toss to coat the wings evenly.

4. Arrange the chicken wings on a baking sheet lined with parchment paper or aluminum foil.

5. Bake in the preheated oven for 35-40 minutes, flipping halfway through, or until the chicken wings are cooked through and golden brown.

6. While the wings are baking, heat vegetable oil in a small saucepan over medium heat. Add the remaining teriyaki sauce and simmer for a few minutes until slightly thickened.

7. Once the chicken wings are cooked, remove them from the oven and brush them with the thickened teriyaki sauce.

8. Garnish with sliced green onions and sesame seeds.

9. Serve hot with cooked rice and steamed broccoli on the side, if desired.

10. Enjoy your homemade Teriyaki Chicken Wings!

Calories	Servings	Prep Time	Cook Time
250	4	10M	40M

INGREDIENTS:

- 2 pounds chicken wings
- 1/4 cup soy sauce
- 2 tablespoons mirin (Japanese sweet rice wine)
- 2 tablespoons sake (or dry sherry)
- 2 tablespoons brown sugar
- 2 cloves garlic, minced
- 1 teaspoon grated ginger
- 1 tablespoon vegetable oil
- Sliced green onions, for garnish
- Sesame seeds, for garnish
- Cooked rice, for serving
- Steamed broccoli, for serving (optional)

Calories	Servings	Prep Time	Cook Time
120	4	20M	15M

INGREDIENTS:

- 4 large portobello mushrooms
- 1/4 cup soy sauce
- 2 tablespoons mirin (Japanese sweet rice wine)
- 2 tablespoons sake (or dry sherry)
- 2 tablespoons brown sugar
- 2 cloves garlic, minced
- 1 teaspoon grated ginger
- 1 tablespoon vegetable oil
- Sliced green onions, for garnish
- Sesame seeds, for garnish
- Cooked rice, for serving
- Steamed broccoli, for serving (optional)

DIRECTIONS:

1. Clean the portobello mushrooms and remove the stems.

2. In a bowl, mix together soy sauce, mirin, sake, brown sugar, minced garlic, and grated ginger to make the teriyaki sauce.

3. Place the mushrooms in a shallow dish and pour half of the teriyaki sauce over them. Allow them to marinate for at least 15 minutes.

4. Heat vegetable oil in a grill pan or skillet over medium-high heat.

5. Place the mushrooms in the pan and cook for 5-6 minutes on each side, or until they are tender and juicy.

6. While the mushrooms are cooking, transfer the remaining teriyaki sauce to a small saucepan and simmer until slightly thickened.

7. Once the mushrooms are cooked, remove them from the pan and brush them with the thickened teriyaki sauce.

8. Garnish with sliced green onions and sesame seeds.

9. Serve hot with cooked rice and steamed broccoli on the side, if desired.

10. Enjoy your homemade Teriyaki Portobello Mushrooms!

DIRECTIONS:

1. Preheat your oven to 400°F (200°C).

2. In a bowl, mix together soy sauce, mirin, sake, brown sugar, minced garlic, and grated ginger to make the teriyaki sauce.

3. Place the sweet potato cubes in a baking dish and pour half of the teriyaki sauce over them. Toss to coat evenly.

4. Bake in the preheated oven for 20-25 minutes, or until the sweet potatoes are tender and caramelized, stirring halfway through.

5. While the sweet potatoes are baking, transfer the remaining teriyaki sauce to a small saucepan and simmer until slightly thickened.

6. Once the sweet potatoes are cooked, remove them from the oven and drizzle with the thickened teriyaki sauce.

7. Garnish with sesame seeds and sliced green onions.

8. Serve hot with cooked rice and steamed broccoli on the side, if desired.

9. Enjoy your homemade Teriyaki Sweet Potato!

Calories	Servings	Prep Time	Cook Time
160	4	15M	25M

INGREDIENTS:

- 2 large sweet potatoes, peeled and cut into cubes
- 1/4 cup soy sauce
- 2 tablespoons mirin (Japanese sweet rice wine)
- 2 tablespoons sake (or dry sherry)
- 2 tablespoons brown sugar
- 2 cloves garlic, minced
- 1 teaspoon grated ginger
- 1 tablespoon vegetable oil
- Sesame seeds, for garnish
- Sliced green onions, for garnish
- Cooked rice, for serving
- Steamed broccoli, for serving (optional)

Calories	Servings	Prep Time	Cook Time
80	4	15M	10M

INGREDIENTS:

- 2 medium zucchinis, sliced into rounds or strips
- 1/4 cup soy sauce
- 2 tablespoons mirin (Japanese sweet rice wine)
- 2 tablespoons sake (or dry sherry)
- 2 tablespoons brown sugar
- 2 cloves garlic, minced
- 1 teaspoon grated ginger
- 1 tablespoon vegetable oil
- Sesame seeds, for garnish
- Sliced green onions, for garnish
- Cooked rice, for serving
- Steamed carrots, for serving (optional)

DIRECTIONS:

1. In a bowl, mix together soy sauce, mirin, sake, brown sugar, minced garlic, and grated ginger to make the teriyaki sauce.

2. Heat vegetable oil in a large skillet or wok over medium-high heat.

3. Add the zucchini slices to the skillet and stir-fry for 3-4 minutes, or until they start to soften.

4. Pour the teriyaki sauce over the zucchini slices and continue to stir-fry for another 2-3 minutes, until the zucchini is tender and coated in the sauce.

5. Remove from heat and transfer the teriyaki zucchini to a serving dish.

6. Garnish with sesame seeds and sliced green onions.

7. Serve hot with cooked rice and steamed carrots on the side, if desired.

8. Enjoy your homemade Teriyaki Zucchini!

DIRECTIONS:

1. In a mixing bowl, combine the chopped kimchi, ground pork or chicken, minced garlic, grated ginger, chopped green onions, soy sauce, sesame oil, sugar, salt, and black pepper. Mix well until all ingredients are thoroughly combined.

2. Take a gyoza wrapper and place a spoonful of the kimchi mixture in the center.

3. Moisten the edges of the wrapper with water and fold it in half, pressing the edges firmly to seal. You can crimp the edges for a decorative touch, if desired. Repeat with the remaining wrappers and filling.

4. Heat vegetable oil in a large skillet or frying pan over medium heat.

5. Place the gyoza in the skillet, flat side down, and cook until the bottoms are golden brown, about 2-3 minutes.

6. Carefully pour water into the skillet, cover with a lid, and steam the gyoza for about 5 minutes, or until the wrappers are translucent and the filling is cooked through.

7. Remove the lid and continue to cook until the water evaporates and the bottoms of the gyoza become crispy again, about 2-3 minutes.

8. Transfer the cooked gyoza to a serving plate and serve hot with soy sauce for dipping.

9. Enjoy your delicious Kimchi Gyoza!

Calories	Servings	Prep Time	Cook Time
120	4	30M	15M

INGREDIENTS:

- 1 cup finely chopped kimchi
- 200g ground pork or chicken
- 2 cloves garlic, minced
- 1 teaspoon grated ginger
- 2 green onions, finely chopped
- 1 tablespoon soy sauce
- 1 teaspoon sesame oil
- 1/2 teaspoon sugar
- 1/4 teaspoon salt
- 1/4 teaspoon black pepper
- 24 gyoza wrappers
- 2 tablespoons vegetable oil
- 1/4 cup water
- Soy sauce, for dipping

Calories	Servings	Prep Time	Cook Time
140	4	45M	15M

INGREDIENTS:

- 200g ground pork
- 1 cup chopped kimchi
- 2 green onions, finely chopped
- 2 cloves garlic, minced
- 1 teaspoon grated ginger
- 1 tablespoon soy sauce
- 1 teaspoon sesame oil
- 24 gyoza wrappers
- 2 tablespoons vegetable oil
- 1/4 cup water
- Soy sauce, for dipping

DIRECTIONS:

1. In a mixing bowl, combine the ground pork, chopped kimchi, chopped green onions, minced garlic, grated ginger, soy sauce, and sesame oil. Mix well until all ingredients are thoroughly combined.

2. Take a gyoza wrapper and place a spoonful of the pork and kimchi mixture in the center.

3. Moisten the edges of the wrapper with water and fold it in half, pressing the edges firmly to seal. You can crimp the edges for a decorative touch, if desired. Repeat with the remaining wrappers and filling.

4. Heat vegetable oil in a large skillet or frying pan over medium heat.

5. Place the gyoza in the skillet, flat side down, and cook until the bottoms are golden brown, about 2-3 minutes.

6. Carefully pour water into the skillet, cover with a lid, and steam the gyoza for about 5 minutes, or until the wrappers are translucent and the filling is cooked through.

7. Remove the lid and continue to cook until the water evaporates and the bottoms of the gyoza become crispy again, about 2-3 minutes.

8. Transfer the cooked gyoza to a serving plate and serve hot with soy sauce for dipping.

9. Enjoy your delicious Pork and Kimchi Gyoza!

DIRECTIONS:

1. In a mixing bowl, combine the crumbled tofu, chopped mixed vegetables, chopped green onions, minced garlic, grated ginger, soy sauce, and sesame oil. Mix well until all ingredients are thoroughly combined.

2. Take a gyoza wrapper and place a spoonful of the tofu and vegetable mixture in the center.

3. Moisten the edges of the wrapper with water and fold it in half, pressing the edges firmly to seal. You can crimp the edges for a decorative touch, if desired. Repeat with the remaining wrappers and filling.

4. Heat vegetable oil in a large skillet or frying pan over medium heat.

5. Place the gyoza in the skillet, flat side down, and cook until the bottoms are golden brown, about 2-3 minutes.

6. Carefully pour water into the skillet, cover with a lid, and steam the gyoza for about 5 minutes, or until the wrappers are translucent and the filling is cooked through.

7. Remove the lid and continue to cook until the water evaporates and the bottoms of the gyoza become crispy again, about 2-3 minutes.

8. Transfer the cooked gyoza to a serving plate and serve hot with soy sauce for dipping.

9. Enjoy your delicious Vegetable and Tofu Gyoza!

Calories	Servings	Prep Time	Cook Time
100	4	45M	15M

INGREDIENTS:

- 1 cup firm tofu, drained and crumbled
- 1 cup finely chopped mixed vegetables (such as cabbage, carrots, and mushrooms)
- 2 green onions, finely chopped
- 2 cloves garlic, minced
- 1 teaspoon grated ginger
- 1 tablespoon soy sauce
- 1 teaspoon sesame oil
- 24 gyoza wrappers
- 2 tablespoons vegetable oil
- 1/4 cup water
- Soy sauce, for dipping

Calories	Servings	Prep Time	Cook Time
140	4	35M	15M

INGREDIENTS:

- 1/2 pound shrimp, peeled and deveined
- 1/2 pound scallops
- 2 green onions, finely chopped
- 2 cloves garlic, minced
- 1 teaspoon grated ginger
- 1 tablespoon soy sauce
- 1 teaspoon sesame oil
- 1 tablespoon vegetable oil
- 24 gyoza wrappers
- 1/4 cup water
- Soy sauce, for dipping

DIRECTIONS:

1. Chop the shrimp and scallops into small pieces and place them in a mixing bowl.

2. Add the chopped green onions, minced garlic, grated ginger, soy sauce, and sesame oil to the bowl with the seafood. Mix well to combine.

3. Take a gyoza wrapper and place a spoonful of the seafood mixture in the center.

4. Moisten the edges of the wrapper with water and fold it in half, pressing the edges firmly to seal. Repeat with the remaining wrappers and filling.

5. Heat vegetable oil in a large skillet or frying pan over medium heat.

6. Place the gyoza in the skillet, flat side down, and cook until the bottoms are golden brown, about 2-3 minutes.

7. Carefully pour water into the skillet, cover with a lid, and steam the gyoza for about 5 minutes, or until the wrappers are translucent and the filling is cooked through.

8. Remove the lid and continue to cook until the water evaporates and the bottoms of the gyoza become crispy again, about 2-3 minutes.

9. Transfer the cooked gyoza to a serving plate and serve hot with soy sauce for dipping.

10. Enjoy your delicious Seafood Gyoza!

DIRECTIONS:

1. In a mixing bowl, combine the ground pork, minced garlic, chopped green onions, soy sauce, and sesame oil. Mix well until evenly combined.

2. Take a gyoza wrapper and place a spoonful of the pork mixture in the center.

3. Moisten the edges of the wrapper with water and fold it in half, pressing the edges firmly to seal. Repeat with the remaining wrappers and filling.

4. Heat vegetable oil in a large skillet or frying pan over medium heat.

5. Place the gyoza in the skillet, flat side down, and cook until the bottoms are golden brown, about 2-3 minutes.

6. Carefully pour water into the skillet, cover with a lid, and steam the gyoza for about 5 minutes, or until the wrappers are translucent and the filling is cooked through.

7. Remove the lid and continue to cook until the water evaporates and the bottoms of the gyoza become crispy again, about 2-3 minutes.

8. Transfer the cooked gyoza to a serving plate and serve hot with soy sauce for dipping.

9. Enjoy your flavorful Garlic Gyoza!

Calories	Servings	Prep Time	Cook Time
180	4	25M	15M

INGREDIENTS:

- 1/2 pound ground pork
- 3 cloves garlic, minced
- 2 green onions, finely chopped
- 1 tablespoon soy sauce
- 1 teaspoon sesame oil
- 24 gyoza wrappers
- 2 tablespoons vegetable oil
- 1/4 cup water
- Soy sauce, for dipping

Calories	Servings	Prep Time	Cook Time
120	4	15M	15M

INGREDIENTS:

- 1 pound chicken tails
- 1/4 cup soy sauce
- 1/4 cup mirin (Japanese sweet rice wine)
- 2 tablespoons sake (Japanese rice wine) or dry white wine
- 2 tablespoons sugar
- Bamboo skewers, soaked in water for 30 minutes
- Green onions, chopped (for garnish)
- Sesame seeds (for garnish)

DIRECTIONS:

1. In a small saucepan, combine the soy sauce, mirin, sake, and sugar. Heat over medium heat until the sugar dissolves, stirring occasionally. Remove from heat and let it cool.

2. Thread the chicken tails onto the bamboo skewers, leaving a little space between each piece.

3. Preheat your grill or broiler to medium-high heat.

4. Brush the chicken tails with the prepared sauce, coating them evenly.

5. Grill or broil the skewers, turning occasionally and brushing with more sauce, until the chicken is cooked through and slightly charred, about 10-12 minutes.

6. Transfer the cooked chicken tail yakitori to a serving platter.

7. Garnish with chopped green onions and sesame seeds.

8. Serve hot and enjoy your delicious Chicken Tail Yakitori!

DIRECTIONS:

1. In a small saucepan, combine the soy sauce, mirin, sake, and sugar. Heat over medium heat until the sugar dissolves, stirring occasionally. Remove from heat and let it cool.

2. Thread the beef rib pieces onto the bamboo skewers, leaving a little space between each piece.

3. Preheat your grill or broiler to medium-high heat.

4. Brush the beef rib yakitori with the prepared sauce, coating them evenly.

5. Grill or broil the skewers, turning occasionally and brushing with more sauce, until the beef ribs are cooked through and slightly charred, about 8-10 minutes.

6. Transfer the cooked beef rib yakitori to a serving platter.

7. Garnish with sliced green onions and sesame seeds.

8. Serve hot and enjoy your delicious Beef Rib Yakitori!

Calories	Servings	Prep Time	Cook Time
180	4	20M	10M

INGREDIENTS:

- 1 pound beef ribs, cut into 1-inch pieces
- 1/4 cup soy sauce
- 1/4 cup mirin (Japanese sweet rice wine)
- 2 tablespoons sake (Japanese rice wine) or dry white wine
- 2 tablespoons sugar
- Bamboo skewers, soaked in water for 30 minutes
- Green onions, sliced (for garnish)
- Sesame seeds (for garnish)

Calories	Servings	Prep Time	Cook Time
80	4	15M	10M

INGREDIENTS:

- 1 bunch asparagus, tough ends trimmed
- 2 tablespoons soy sauce
- 2 tablespoons mirin (Japanese sweet rice wine)
- 1 tablespoon sake (Japanese rice wine) or dry white wine
- 1 tablespoon brown sugar
- Bamboo skewers, soaked in water for 30 minutes
- Sesame seeds (for garnish)
- Lemon wedges (for serving)

DIRECTIONS:

1. In a small saucepan, combine the soy sauce, mirin, sake, and brown sugar. Heat over medium heat until the sugar dissolves, stirring occasionally. Remove from heat and let it cool.

2. Thread the trimmed asparagus spears onto the bamboo skewers, leaving a little space between each piece.

3. Preheat your grill or broiler to medium-high heat.

4. Brush the asparagus yakitori with the prepared sauce, coating them evenly.

5. Grill or broil the skewers, turning occasionally and brushing with more sauce, until the asparagus is tender and slightly charred, about 8-10 minutes.

6. Transfer the cooked asparagus yakitori to a serving platter.

7. Garnish with sesame seeds.

8. Serve hot with lemon wedges on the side.

9. Enjoy your flavorful Asparagus Yakitori!

DIRECTIONS:

1. Clean the mushrooms and remove the stems if necessary. Thread the mushrooms onto the bamboo skewers, leaving a little space between each mushroom.

2. In a small saucepan, combine the soy sauce, mirin, sake, and brown sugar. Heat over medium heat until the sugar dissolves, stirring occasionally. Remove from heat and let it cool.

3. Preheat your grill or broiler to medium-high heat.

4. Brush the mushroom yakitori with the prepared sauce, coating them evenly.

5. Grill or broil the skewers, turning occasionally and brushing with more sauce, until the mushrooms are tender and slightly charred, about 5-7 minutes.

6. Transfer the cooked mushroom yakitori to a serving platter.

7. Garnish with sesame seeds and thinly sliced green onions.

8. Serve hot and enjoy your Mushroom Yakitori!

Calories	Servings	Prep Time	Cook Time
80	4	15M	10M

INGREDIENTS:

- 1 pound mixed mushrooms (such as shiitake, cremini, and button mushrooms)
- 2 tablespoons soy sauce
- 2 tablespoons mirin (Japanese sweet rice wine)
- 1 tablespoon sake (Japanese rice wine) or dry white wine
- 1 tablespoon brown sugar
- Bamboo skewers, soaked in water for 30 minutes
- Sesame seeds (for garnish)
- Green onions, thinly sliced (for garnish)

GARLIC YAKITORI
YAKITORI

Calories	Servings	Prep Time	Cook Time
80	4	15M	10M

INGREDIENTS:

- 1 lb boneless, skinless chicken thighs, cut into bite-sized pieces
- 8 cloves garlic, peeled
- 2 tablespoons soy sauce
- 2 tablespoons mirin (Japanese sweet rice wine)
- 1 tablespoon sake (Japanese rice wine) or dry white wine
- 1 tablespoon brown sugar
- Bamboo skewers, soaked in water for 30 minutes
- Vegetable oil (for grilling)
- Thinly sliced green onions (for garnish)

DIRECTIONS:

1. In a bowl, combine the soy sauce, mirin, sake, and brown sugar. Stir until the sugar is dissolved.

2. Add the chicken pieces to the marinade, making sure they are well coated. Let marinate for at least 30 minutes, or up to 2 hours in the refrigerator.

3. Preheat your grill or broiler to medium-high heat.

4. Thread the marinated chicken pieces and garlic cloves alternately onto the bamboo skewers.

5. Brush the grill grates lightly with vegetable oil to prevent sticking.

6. Place the skewers on the grill or under the broiler, and cook for 4-5 minutes on each side, or until the chicken is cooked through and has a nice char.

7. While grilling, brush the skewers with the remaining marinade to keep them moist and flavorful.

8. Transfer the cooked yakitori to a serving platter and garnish with thinly sliced green onions.

9. Serve hot and enjoy your Garlic Yakitori!

DIRECTIONS:

1. In a large mixing bowl, combine the all-purpose flour, dashi stock or chicken broth, and eggs. Whisk until smooth.

2. Add the shredded cabbage, green onions, cooked shrimp, cooked squid (if using), tenkasu or panko breadcrumbs, pickled ginger, and chopped cilantro (if using) to the batter. Mix until well combined. Season with salt and pepper to taste.

3. Heat a non-stick skillet or griddle over medium heat. Add a little vegetable oil to coat the surface.

4. Pour a portion of the batter onto the skillet to form a round pancake, about 6 inches in diameter. Cook for 3-4 minutes, or until the bottom is golden brown and crispy.

5. Carefully flip the okonomiyaki using a spatula, and cook for an additional 3-4 minutes on the other side, until cooked through and crispy.

6. Transfer the cooked okonomiyaki to a serving plate. Drizzle with okonomiyaki sauce or tonkatsu sauce, Japanese mayonnaise, and sprinkle with bonito flakes.

7. Repeat the process with the remaining batter to make more okonomiyaki.

8. Serve hot and enjoy your Modern Okonomiyaki with Mayo and Bonito Flakes!

Calories	Servings	Prep Time	Cook Time
350	4	15M	15M

INGREDIENTS:

- 2 cups all-purpose flour
- 1 cup dashi stock or chicken broth
- 2 large eggs
- 2 cups shredded cabbage
- 4 green onions, thinly sliced
- 1 cup cooked shrimp, chopped (optional)
- 1 cup cooked squid, chopped (optional)
- 1/2 cup tenkasu (tempura scraps) or panko breadcrumbs
- 1/4 cup pickled ginger, chopped
- 1/4 cup chopped fresh cilantro (optional)
- 1/4 cup okonomiyaki sauce or tonkatsu sauce
- 1/4 cup Japanese mayonnaise
- 1/4 cup bonito flakes
- Vegetable oil, for frying
- Salt and pepper, to taste

Calories	Servings	Prep Time	Cook Time
350	4	20M	15M

INGREDIENTS:

- 2 cups all-purpose flour
- 1 cup dashi stock or chicken broth
- 2 large eggs
- 2 cups shredded cabbage
- 1 cup mixed seafood (shrimp, squid, scallops), chopped
- 4 green onions, thinly sliced
- 1/2 cup tenkasu (tempura scraps) or panko breadcrumbs
- 1/4 cup pickled ginger, chopped
- 1/4 cup okonomiyaki sauce or tonkatsu sauce
- 1/4 cup Japanese mayonnaise
- Vegetable oil, for frying
- Salt and pepper, to taste

DIRECTIONS:

1. In a large mixing bowl, combine the all-purpose flour, dashi stock or chicken broth, and eggs. Whisk until smooth.

2. Add the shredded cabbage, mixed seafood, green onions, tenkasu or panko breadcrumbs, and pickled ginger to the batter. Mix until well combined. Season with salt and pepper to taste.

3. Heat a non-stick skillet or griddle over medium heat. Add a little vegetable oil to coat the surface.

4. Pour a portion of the batter onto the skillet to form a round pancake, about 6 inches in diameter. Cook for 3-4 minutes, or until the bottom is golden brown and crispy.

5. Carefully flip the okonomiyaki using a spatula, and cook for an additional 3-4 minutes on the other side, until cooked through and crispy.

6. Transfer the cooked okonomiyaki to a serving plate. Drizzle with okonomiyaki sauce or tonkatsu sauce, Japanese mayonnaise, and sprinkle with additional chopped green onions and bonito flakes if desired.

7. Repeat the process with the remaining batter to make more okonomiyaki.

8. Serve hot and enjoy your Okonomiyaki with Seafood!

Directions:

1. In a large mixing bowl, combine the all-purpose flour, vegetable or chicken broth, and eggs. Whisk until smooth.

2. Add the shredded cabbage, grated carrot, chopped kale or spinach, sliced mushrooms, chopped green onions, and tenkasu or panko breadcrumbs to the batter. Mix until well combined. Season with salt and pepper to taste.

3. Heat a non-stick skillet or griddle over medium heat. Add a little vegetable oil to coat the surface.

4. Pour a portion of the batter onto the skillet to form a round pancake, about 6 inches in diameter. Cook for 3-4 minutes, or until the bottom is golden brown and crispy.

5. Carefully flip the okonomiyaki using a spatula, and cook for an additional 3-4 minutes on the other side, until cooked through and crispy.

6. Transfer the cooked okonomiyaki to a serving plate. Drizzle with okonomiyaki sauce or tonkatsu sauce, Japanese mayonnaise, and sprinkle with additional chopped green onions if desired.

7. Repeat the process with the remaining batter to make more okonomiyaki.

8. Serve hot and enjoy your Okonomiyaki with Vegetables!

Calories	Servings	Prep Time	Cook Time
350	4	20M	15M

Ingredients:

- 2 cups all-purpose flour
- 1 cup vegetable or chicken broth
- 2 large eggs
- 2 cups shredded cabbage
- 1 carrot, grated
- 1/2 cup chopped kale or spinach
- 1/2 cup sliced mushrooms (shiitake or button)
- 1/4 cup chopped green onions
- 1/4 cup tenkasu (tempura scraps) or panko breadcrumbs
- 1/4 cup okonomiyaki sauce or tonkatsu sauce
- 1/4 cup Japanese mayonnaise
- Vegetable oil, for frying
- Salt and pepper, to taste

Calories	Servings	Prep Time	Cook Time
320	4	25M	15M

INGREDIENTS:

- 2 cups all-purpose flour
- 1 1/2 cups dashi broth or chicken broth
- 2 large eggs
- 2 cups shredded cabbage
- 1/2 cup thinly sliced green onions
- 1/4 cup tenkasu (tempura scraps) or panko breadcrumbs
- 1/4 cup pickled red ginger (beni shoga)
- 1/4 cup bonito flakes
- 1/4 cup okonomiyaki sauce or tonkatsu sauce
- 1/4 cup Japanese mayonnaise
- 1/4 cup mentaiko (spicy pollock roe), optional for topping
- Vegetable oil, for frying
- Salt and pepper, to taste

DIRECTIONS:

1. In a large mixing bowl, combine the all-purpose flour, dashi broth or chicken broth, and eggs. Whisk until smooth.

2. Add the shredded cabbage, sliced green onions, tenkasu or panko breadcrumbs, and pickled red ginger to the batter. Season with salt and pepper to taste. Mix until well combined.

3. Heat a non-stick skillet or griddle over medium heat. Add a little vegetable oil to coat the surface.

4. Pour a portion of the batter onto the skillet to form a round pancake, about 6 inches in diameter. Cook for 3-4 minutes, or until the bottom is golden brown and crispy.

5. Carefully flip the okonomiyaki using a spatula, and cook for an additional 3-4 minutes on the other side, until cooked through and crispy.

6. Transfer the cooked okonomiyaki to a serving plate. Drizzle with okonomiyaki sauce or tonkatsu sauce, Japanese mayonnaise, and sprinkle with bonito flakes.

7. If desired, top the okonomiyaki with a spoonful of mentaiko (spicy pollock roe).

8. Serve hot and enjoy your Okonomiyaki with Mentaiko!

DIRECTIONS:

1. In a large mixing bowl, combine the all-purpose flour, dashi broth or chicken broth, and eggs. Whisk until smooth.

2. Add the shredded cabbage and tempura bits (tenkasu) to the batter. Season with salt and pepper to taste. Mix until well combined.

3. Heat a non-stick skillet or griddle over medium heat. Add a little vegetable oil to coat the surface.

4. Pour a portion of the batter onto the skillet to form a round pancake, about 6 inches in diameter. Cook for 3-4 minutes, or until the bottom is golden brown and crispy.

5. Carefully flip the okonomiyaki using a spatula, and cook for an additional 3-4 minutes on the other side, until cooked through and crispy.

6. Transfer the cooked okonomiyaki to a serving plate. Drizzle with okonomiyaki sauce or tonkatsu sauce, Japanese mayonnaise, and sprinkle with bonito flakes.

7. Serve hot and enjoy your Okonomiyaki with Tempura Bits!

Calories	Servings	Prep Time	Cook Time
320	4	20M	15M

INGREDIENTS:

- 2 cups all-purpose flour
- 1 1/2 cups dashi broth or chicken broth
- 2 large eggs
- 2 cups shredded cabbage
- 1/4 cup tempura bits (tenkasu) or panko breadcrumbs
- 1/4 cup bonito flakes
- 1/4 cup okonomiyaki sauce or tonkatsu sauce
- 1/4 cup Japanese mayonnaise
- Vegetable oil, for frying
- Salt and pepper, to taste

Calories	Servings	Prep Time	Cook Time
250	4	15M	10M

INGREDIENTS:

- 8 cups water
- 14 oz (400g) Sanuki udon noodles
- 4 cups dashi broth or vegetable broth
- 1/4 cup soy sauce
- 2 tablespoons mirin (Japanese sweet rice wine)
- 2 tablespoons sake (Japanese rice wine)
- 1 tablespoon sugar
- 1 cup sliced green onions
- 4 pieces narutomaki (fish cake), sliced
- 4 pieces kamaboko (fish cake), sliced
- 1 cup shredded nori (seaweed)
- Optional toppings: thinly sliced cooked chicken, boiled egg, tempura flakes, sliced mushrooms

DIRECTIONS:

1. In a large pot, bring the water to a boil. Add the udon noodles and cook according to the package instructions until al dente. Drain and rinse the noodles under cold water to stop the cooking process. Set aside.

2. In another pot, combine the dashi broth, soy sauce, mirin, sake, and sugar. Bring to a simmer over medium heat and let it cook for 5 minutes to allow the flavors to meld together.

3. Divide the cooked udon noodles among four serving bowls.

4. Ladle the hot broth over the noodles in each bowl.

5. Arrange the sliced green onions, narutomaki, kamaboko, and shredded nori on top of each bowl.

6. Add any optional toppings you desire, such as thinly sliced cooked chicken, boiled egg, tempura flakes, or sliced mushrooms.

7. Serve hot and enjoy your Sanuki Udon!

DIRECTIONS:

1. Cook the udon noodles according to the package instructions. Drain and set aside.

2. In a large pot, bring the dashi stock to a simmer over medium heat.

3. Stir in the soy sauce, mirin, and sugar. Let the broth simmer for a few minutes to allow the flavors to meld together.

4. Divide the cooked udon noodles among serving bowls.

5. Ladle the hot broth over the noodles, ensuring each bowl gets an equal amount of broth.

6. Top each bowl of Kake Udon with a generous amount of tempura bits.

7. Garnish with sliced green onions, shichimi togarashi, and nori strips, if desired.

8. Serve immediately and enjoy your comforting bowl of Kake Udon with Tempura Bits!

Calories	Servings	Prep Time	Cook Time
280	4	10M	20M

INGREDIENTS:

- 8 oz (225g) udon noodles
- 4 cups dashi stock (or vegetable broth)
- 4 tablespoons soy sauce
- 2 tablespoons mirin (Japanese sweet rice wine)
- 1 tablespoon sugar
- 1 cup tempura bits (store-bought or homemade)
- 2 green onions, thinly sliced
- Shichimi togarashi (Japanese seven spice blend), for garnish (optional)
- Nori (dried seaweed), sliced into thin strips, for garnish (optional)

Calories	Servings	Prep Time	Cook Time
340	4	10M	20M

INGREDIENTS:

- 8 oz (225g) udon noodles
- 4 cups vegetable or chicken broth
- 1/4 cup soy sauce
- 2 tablespoons mirin (Japanese sweet rice wine)
- 2 tablespoons sugar
- 2 tablespoons sesame seeds
- Optional toppings: sliced green onions, cooked shrimp, shredded nori (seaweed), steamed vegetables

DIRECTIONS:

1. Cook the udon noodles according to the package instructions. Drain and set aside.

2. In a large pot, bring the vegetable or chicken broth to a simmer over medium heat.

3. Stir in the soy sauce, mirin, and sugar. Let the broth simmer for a few minutes to blend the flavors.

4. Add the cooked udon noodles to the pot and let them heat through in the broth for about 1-2 minutes.

5. Divide the udon and broth into serving bowls.

6. Sprinkle each bowl with sesame seeds.

7. Optionally, top with sliced green onions, cooked shrimp, shredded nori, or steamed vegetables.

8. Serve hot and enjoy your delicious Udon with Sesame Seeds! Adjust toppings according to preference.

DIRECTIONS:

1. Cook the soba noodles according to the package instructions. Drain and rinse under cold water. Set aside.

2. In a large skillet, heat the vegetable oil over medium-high heat. Add the diced eggplant and season with salt and pepper. Sauté until the eggplant is tender and golden brown, about 8-10 minutes. Remove from heat and set aside.

3. In a food processor, combine the toasted walnuts, soy sauce, mirin, rice vinegar, sesame oil, garlic, and ginger. Process until smooth, adding a little water if necessary to achieve a creamy consistency.

4. In a large bowl, toss the cooked soba noodles with the walnut sauce until evenly coated.

5. Add the sautéed eggplant and green onions to the noodles, gently tossing to combine.

6. Serve the soba noodles with eggplant and walnut sauce at room temperature or slightly chilled. Adjust seasonings if needed.<p>Enjoy your Soba with Eggplant and Walnut Sauce!</p>

Calories	Servings	Prep Time	Cook Time
400	4	20M	25M

INGREDIENTS:

- 8 oz (225g) soba noodles
- 1 large eggplant, diced
- 1 cup walnuts, toasted
- 1/4 cup soy sauce
- 2 tablespoons mirin (Japanese sweet rice wine)
- 2 tablespoons rice vinegar
- 1 tablespoon sesame oil
- 1 garlic clove, minced
- 1 tablespoon ginger, grated
- 2 green onions, sliced
- 1 tablespoon vegetable oil
- Salt and pepper to taste

Calories	Servings	Prep Time	Cook Time
400	4	20M	10M

INGREDIENTS:

- 8 oz (225g) soba noodles
- 1/4 cup tahini (sesame paste)
- 3 tablespoons soy sauce
- 2 tablespoons rice vinegar
- 1 tablespoon sesame oil
- 1 tablespoon honey or agave syrup
- 1 garlic clove, minced
- 1 teaspoon grated ginger
- 1/2 cup water
- 1 cucumber, julienned
- 1 carrot, julienned
- 2 green onions, sliced
- 1/4 cup toasted sesame seeds
- 1 avocado, sliced (optional)
- Sliced radishes (optional)
- Chopped cilantro (optional)

DIRECTIONS:

1. Cook the soba noodles according to the package instructions. Drain and rinse under cold water to stop the cooking process. Set aside.

2. In a medium bowl, whisk together the tahini, soy sauce, rice vinegar, sesame oil, honey (or agave syrup), garlic, and ginger. Gradually add the water, whisking until the dressing is smooth and creamy.

3. In a large bowl, combine the cooked soba noodles, cucumber, carrot, and green onions.

4. Pour the creamy sesame dressing over the noodle mixture and toss until everything is well coated.

5. Divide the soba mixture among serving bowls. Top with toasted sesame seeds.

6. If desired, add avocado slices, radishes, and cilantro as additional toppings.

7. Serve the soba salad chilled.<p>Enjoy your Cold Creamy Sesame Soba!</p>

DIRECTIONS:

1. Cook the soba noodles according to package instructions. Drain and rinse under cold water to stop the cooking process. Set aside.

2. Heat vegetable oil in a large pot or skillet over medium heat. Add minced garlic and ginger, sautéing until fragrant, about 1 minute.

3. Add the sliced shiitake and cremini mushrooms to the pot. Cook until the mushrooms are tender and have released their moisture, about 5 minutes.

4. Add the fresh spinach leaves to the pot, stirring until wilted, about 2 minutes.

5. Pour in the vegetable broth, soy sauce, mirin, and sake (if using). Bring to a simmer and cook for an additional 3-4 minutes to allow the flavors to meld.

6. Add the cooked soba noodles to the pot, gently stirring to combine and heat through.

7. Drizzle the sesame oil over the soba and mix well.

8. Serve the soba in bowls, garnished with thinly sliced green onions and a sprinkle of sesame seeds.

9. Enjoy your warm and nourishing bowl of Soba with Mushrooms and Spinach.

Calories	Servings	Prep Time	Cook Time
350	4	15M	15M

INGREDIENTS:

- 8 oz soba noodles
- 1 tablespoon vegetable oil
- 2 cloves garlic, minced
- 1 tablespoon ginger, minced
- 1 cup shiitake mushrooms, sliced
- 1 cup cremini mushrooms, sliced
- 4 cups fresh spinach leaves
- 4 cups vegetable broth
- 2 tablespoons soy sauce
- 1 tablespoon mirin (Japanese sweet rice wine)
- 1 tablespoon sake (optional)
- 1 teaspoon sesame oil
- 2 green onions, thinly sliced
- Sesame seeds for garnish

Calories	Servings	Prep Time	Cook Time
350	4	15M	15M

INGREDIENTS:

- 8 oz soba noodles
- 1 lb shrimp, peeled and deveined
- 4 cups dashi stock (or low-sodium chicken broth)
- 2 tablespoons soy sauce
- 1 tablespoon mirin (Japanese sweet rice wine)
- 1 tablespoon sake (optional)
- 2 tablespoons fresh ginger, grated
- 2 cloves garlic, minced
- 2 green onions, sliced
- 1 tablespoon sesame oil
- 1/2 cup mushrooms, sliced (shiitake or button mushrooms work well)
- 1 carrot, julienned
- 1 cup spinach leaves
- Salt and pepper to taste
- Lemon wedges (for garnish)
- Toasted sesame seeds (for garnish)

DIRECTIONS:

1. Cook the soba noodles according to package instructions. Drain, rinse under cold water, and set aside.

2. In a large pot, heat the sesame oil over medium heat. Add the grated ginger and minced garlic, and sauté until fragrant, about 1 minute.

3. Pour in the dashi stock (or chicken broth), soy sauce, mirin, and sake (if using). Bring to a gentle boil.

4. Add the sliced mushrooms and julienned carrot to the broth. Cook for about 5 minutes until the vegetables are tender.

5. Add the shrimp to the broth and cook for 3-4 minutes, until the shrimp are pink and cooked through.

6. Season the broth with salt and pepper to taste. Add the spinach leaves and cook until wilted, about 1 minute.

7. Divide the cooked soba noodles into serving bowls. Ladle the shrimp and ginger broth over the noodles.

8. Garnish with sliced green onions, toasted sesame seeds, and lemon wedges. Serve immediately and enjoy the comforting flavors of the shrimp and ginger broth with soba noodles.

DIRECTIONS:

1. Cook the soba noodles according to package instructions. Drain, rinse under cold water, and set aside.

2. In a large skillet or wok, heat the vegetable oil over medium-high heat. Add the minced garlic and grated ginger. Cook for about 1 minute, until fragrant.

3. Add the mixed vegetables to the skillet. Stir-fry for 5-7 minutes, or until the vegetables are tender-crisp.

4. In a small bowl, whisk together the soy sauce, mirin or rice vinegar, and sesame oil. Pour the sauce over the vegetables in the skillet.

5. Add the cooked soba noodles to the skillet. Toss everything together until well combined and heated through, about 2-3 minutes.

6. Season with salt and pepper to taste.

7. Divide the soba noodles and vegetable mixture among serving bowls.

8. Garnish with sliced green onions and sesame seeds.

9. Serve hot and enjoy this delicious and nutritious Soba with Vegetables and Soy Sauce!

Calories	Servings	Prep Time	Cook Time
300	4	15M	15M

INGREDIENTS:

- 8 oz soba noodles
- 2 tablespoons vegetable oil
- 2 cloves garlic, minced
- 1 tablespoon fresh ginger, grated
- 2 cups mixed vegetables (such as bell peppers, carrots, broccoli, and snow peas), thinly sliced or julienned
- 1/4 cup soy sauce
- 2 tablespoons mirin (Japanese sweet rice wine) or rice vinegar
- 1 tablespoon sesame oil
- 2 green onions, thinly sliced (for garnish)
- Sesame seeds (for garnish)
- Salt and pepper to taste

Calories	Servings	Prep Time	Cook Time
500	4	15M	15M

INGREDIENTS:

- 8 oz (225g) yakisoba noodles
- 1 cup kimchi, chopped
- 1/2 lb (225g) pork belly or chicken breast, thinly sliced
- 1/2 onion, thinly sliced
- 1/2 carrot, julienned
- 1/2 bell pepper, thinly sliced
- 2 green onions, chopped
- 2 cloves garlic, minced
- 2 tablespoons soy sauce
- 1 tablespoon oyster sauce
- 1 tablespoon gochujang (Korean red chili paste)
- 1 tablespoon vegetable oil
- 1 teaspoon sesame oil
- Sesame seeds for garnish

DIRECTIONS:

1. Prepare yakisoba noodles according to package instructions. Drain and set aside.

2. Heat vegetable oil in a large skillet or wok over medium-high heat. Add the sliced pork belly or chicken breast and cook until browned.

3. Add the minced garlic and cook for another minute until fragrant.

4. Add the onion, carrot, and bell pepper to the skillet. Stir-fry until the vegetables are tender.

5. Stir in the chopped kimchi and cook for 2 minutes.

6. Add the cooked yakisoba noodles to the skillet, tossing to combine with the meat and vegetables.

7. In a small bowl, mix together the soy sauce, oyster sauce, and gochujang. Pour over the yakisoba and toss to coat evenly.

8. Drizzle with sesame oil and sprinkle with chopped green onions and sesame seeds.

9. Serve hot and enjoy your Spicy Kimchi Yakisoba!

DIRECTIONS:

1. Prepare yakisoba noodles according to package instructions. Drain and set aside.

2. In a small bowl, mix the soy sauce, oyster sauce, Worcestershire sauce, and mirin (if using).

3. In another small bowl, mix the cornstarch with 1/4 cup of water until dissolved. Set aside.

4. Heat 1 tablespoon of vegetable oil in a large skillet or wok over medium-high heat. Add the minced garlic and cook for 1 minute until fragrant.

5. Add the onion and carrot to the skillet and stir-fry for 2-3 minutes until they start to soften.

6. Add the cabbage to the skillet and continue to stir-fry for another 2-3 minutes until slightly wilted.

7. Add the drained tuna to the skillet and break it apart with a spatula.

8. Add the cooked yakisoba noodles to the skillet and pour the sauce mixture over them. Toss to coat evenly.

9. Add the cornstarch mixture to the skillet and cook for another 1-2 minutes until the sauce thickens.

10. Drizzle with sesame oil and sprinkle with chopped green onions and sesame seeds.

11. Serve hot and enjoy your Tuna Yakisoba!

Calories	Servings	Prep Time	Cook Time
450	4	15M	20M

INGREDIENTS:

- 8 oz (225g) yakisoba noodles
- 2 cans (5 oz each) tuna, drained
- 1 cup cabbage, shredded
- 1/2 onion, thinly sliced
- 1 carrot, julienned
- 2 cloves garlic, minced
- 2 green onions, chopped
- 3 tablespoons soy sauce
- 1 tablespoon oyster sauce
- 1 tablespoon Worcestershire sauce
- 1 tablespoon mirin (optional)
- 2 tablespoons vegetable oil
- 1 teaspoon sesame oil
- 1 teaspoon cornstarch
- 1/4 cup water
- Sesame seeds for garnish

Calories	Servings	Prep Time	Cook Time
420	4	15M	20M

INGREDIENTS:

- 8 oz (225g) udon noodles
- 1 bell pepper, thinly sliced
- 1 carrot, julienned
- 1/2 onion, thinly sliced
- 1 cup sliced cabbage
- 1 cup sliced mushrooms (shiitake or cremini)
- 1 cup cooked chicken, sliced
- 2 cloves garlic, minced
- 2 tablespoons vegetable oil
- 3 tablespoons soy sauce
- 2 tablespoons Worcestershire sauce
- 1 tablespoon oyster sauce
- 1 tablespoon ketchup
- Salt and pepper to taste
- Green onions, thinly sliced, for garnish
- Sesame seeds, for garnish

DIRECTIONS:

1. Cook udon noodles according to package instructions. Drain and set aside.

2. In a small bowl, mix together soy sauce, Worcestershire sauce, oyster sauce, and ketchup. Set aside.

3. Heat vegetable oil in a large skillet or wok over medium-high heat. Add minced garlic and cook for 1 minute until fragrant.

4. Add sliced bell pepper, julienned carrot, thinly sliced onion, sliced cabbage, and sliced mushrooms to the skillet. Stir-fry for 2-3 minutes until vegetables start to soften.

5. Add cooked chicken to the skillet and stir-fry for another 2 minutes.

6. Add the cooked udon noodles to the skillet and pour the sauce mixture over them. Toss everything together until well combined.

7. Cook for an additional 2-3 minutes until everything is heated through and the noodles are well coated with the sauce.

8. Season with salt and pepper to taste.

9. Garnish with thinly sliced green onions and sesame seeds.

10. Serve hot and enjoy your Yaki Udon, a delicious crossover dish with Yakisoba!

DIRECTIONS:

1. Cook the yakisoba noodles according to package instructions. Drain and set aside.

2. Heat 1 tablespoon of vegetable oil in a large skillet or wok over medium-high heat. Add the sliced pork and cook until browned and cooked through, about 3-4 minutes. Remove the pork from the skillet and set aside.

3. In the same skillet, add the remaining tablespoon of vegetable oil. Add the minced garlic and cook for about 30 seconds until fragrant.

4. Add the sliced onion to the skillet and cook for 2-3 minutes until softened.

5. Add the shredded cabbage and julienned carrots to the skillet. Stir-fry for another 2-3 minutes until the vegetables are tender-crisp.

6. Return the cooked pork to the skillet.

7. Add the cooked yakisoba noodles to the skillet, along with the yakisoba sauce.

8. Toss everything together until well combined and heated through, about 2-3 minutes.

9. Season with salt and pepper to taste.

10. Divide the yakisoba among serving plates.

11. Garnish with thinly sliced green onions and toasted sesame seeds.

12. Serve hot and enjoy this delicious Pork and Cabbage Yakisoba!

Calories	Servings	Prep Time	Cook Time
420	4	15M	15M

INGREDIENTS:

- 8 oz yakisoba noodles (or substitute with spaghetti)
- 8 oz pork loin or pork belly, thinly sliced
- 2 tablespoons vegetable oil
- 2 cloves garlic, minced
- 1 small onion, thinly sliced
- 4 cups shredded cabbage
- 2 carrots, julienned
- 1/4 cup yakisoba sauce (or substitute with Worcestershire sauce mixed with soy sauce and a touch of sugar)
- Salt and pepper to taste
- Green onions, thinly sliced (for garnish)
- Toasted sesame seeds (for garnish)

Calories	Servings	Prep Time	Cook Time
420	4	15M	15M

INGREDIENTS:

- 8 oz yakisoba noodles (or substitute with spaghetti)
- 2 tablespoons vegetable oil
- 2 cloves garlic, minced
- 1 small onion, thinly sliced
- 1 bell pepper, thinly sliced
- 1 cup shredded cabbage
- 1 carrot, julienned
- 1 cup cooked chicken, shredded (optional)
- 1/4 cup soy sauce
- 2 tablespoons peanut butter
- 1 tablespoon sriracha sauce (adjust to taste)
- 1 tablespoon honey
- 2 tablespoons lime juice
- Salt and pepper to taste
- Chopped peanuts (for garnish)
- Chopped cilantro (for garnish)
- Lime wedges (for serving)

DIRECTIONS:

1. Cook the yakisoba noodles according to package instructions. Drain and set aside.

2. In a small bowl, whisk together soy sauce, peanut butter, sriracha sauce, honey, and lime juice to make the spicy peanut sauce. Set aside.

3. Heat vegetable oil in a large skillet or wok over medium-high heat. Add minced garlic and cook for about 30 seconds until fragrant.

4. Add sliced onion and bell pepper to the skillet. Stir-fry for 2-3 minutes until slightly softened.

5. Add shredded cabbage and julienned carrot to the skillet. Continue to stir-fry for another 2-3 minutes until the vegetables are tender-crisp.

6. If using, add the cooked shredded chicken to the skillet and toss to combine with the vegetables.

7. Add the cooked yakisoba noodles to the skillet.

8. Pour the spicy peanut sauce over the noodles and vegetables. Toss everything together until well coated and heated through.

9. Season with salt and pepper to taste.

10. Divide the spicy peanut sauce yakisoba among serving plates.

11. Garnish with chopped peanuts and chopped cilantro.

12. Serve with lime wedges on the side for an extra burst of flavor.

13. Enjoy your delicious and flavorful Spicy Peanut Sauce Yakisoba!

DIRECTIONS:

1. Cook the yakisoba noodles according to package instructions. Drain and set aside.

2. Heat 1 tablespoon of vegetable oil in a large skillet or wok over medium-high heat. Add the tofu cubes and cook until golden brown on all sides. Remove the tofu from the skillet and set aside.

3. In the same skillet, add the remaining tablespoon of vegetable oil. Add minced garlic and cook for about 30 seconds until fragrant.

4. Add thinly sliced onion to the skillet and cook until softened.

5. Add thinly sliced bell peppers to the skillet and stir-fry for 2-3 minutes until slightly tender.

6. Add shredded cabbage to the skillet and continue to stir-fry until wilted.

7. Add the cooked yakisoba noodles and tofu cubes back to the skillet.

8. In a small bowl, mix together soy sauce, oyster sauce, Worcestershire sauce, and ketchup to make the yakisoba sauce. Pour the sauce over the noodles and vegetables.

9. Toss everything together until well coated and heated through.

10. Season with salt and pepper to taste.

11. Divide the Yakisoba with Tofu and Bell Peppers among serving plates.

12. Garnish with chopped green onions and toasted sesame seeds.

13. Serve with lime wedges on the side.

14. Enjoy your delicious Yakisoba with Tofu and Bell Peppers!

Calories	Servings	Prep Time	Cook Time
320	4	15M	20M

INGREDIENTS:

- 8 oz yakisoba noodles (or substitute with spaghetti)
- 2 tablespoons vegetable oil
- 14 oz firm tofu, pressed and cut into cubes
- 2 cloves garlic, minced
- 1 small onion, thinly sliced
- 2 bell peppers (assorted colors), thinly sliced
- 2 cups shredded cabbage
- 2 tablespoons soy sauce
- 1 tablespoon oyster sauce
- 1 tablespoon Worcestershire sauce
- 1 tablespoon ketchup
- Salt and pepper to taste
- Green onions, chopped (for garnish)
- Toasted sesame seeds (for garnish)
- Lime wedges (for serving)

Calories	Servings	Prep Time	Cook Time
220	4	15M	20M

INGREDIENTS:

- 4 large eggs
- 2 cups chicken or vegetable broth
- 1 tablespoon soy sauce
- 1 tablespoon mirin
- 1/2 teaspoon salt
- 1/2 teaspoon sugar
- 4 slices black truffle (fresh or preserved), thinly sliced
- 4 shiitake mushrooms, thinly sliced
- 4 large shrimp, peeled and deveined
- 4 slices kamaboko (fish cake)
- 4 sprigs parsley or substitute with chives or green onions
- Soy sauce, for serving

DIRECTIONS:

1. In a mixing bowl, whisk together eggs, broth, soy sauce, mirin, salt, and sugar until well combined.

2. Strain the egg mixture through a fine mesh sieve to remove any lumps.

3. Divide the sliced black truffle, shiitake mushrooms, shrimp, and kamaboko evenly among 4 chawanmushi cups or small heatproof bowls.

4. Pour the egg mixture over the ingredients in each cup, filling them almost to the top.

5. Place a sprig of parsley on top of each cup.

6. Prepare a steamer and bring the water to a gentle boil.

7. Carefully place the cups into the steamer basket and cover with a lid.

8. Steam the chawanmushi for about 15-20 minutes until they are just set but still slightly jiggly in the center.

9. Once cooked, remove the chawanmushi from the steamer and let them cool slightly.

10. Serve the Black Truffle Chawanmushi warm with a small dish of soy sauce on the side for dipping. Enjoy this luxurious and aromatic Japanese dish!

DIRECTIONS:

1. In a mixing bowl, whisk together eggs, broth, soy sauce, mirin, salt, and sugar until well combined.

2. Strain the egg mixture through a fine mesh sieve to remove any lumps.

3. Divide the foie gras slices, shiitake mushrooms, ginkgo nuts, carrot slices, and snow peas evenly among 4 chawanmushi cups or small heatproof bowls.

4. Pour the egg mixture over the ingredients in each cup, filling them almost to the top.

5. Place a few mitsuba leaves on top of each cup for garnish.

6. Prepare a steamer and bring the water to a gentle boil.

7. Carefully place the cups into the steamer basket and cover with a lid.

8. Steam the chawanmushi for about 20-25 minutes until they are just set but still slightly jiggly in the center.

9. Once cooked, remove the chawanmushi from the steamer and let them cool slightly.

10. Serve the Foie Gras Chawanmushi warm with a small dish of soy sauce on the side for dipping. Enjoy this luxurious and flavorful Japanese delicacy!

Calories	Servings	Prep Time	Cook Time
320	4	20M	25M

INGREDIENTS:

- 4 large eggs
- 2 cups chicken or vegetable broth
- 1 tablespoon soy sauce
- 1 tablespoon mirin
- 1/2 teaspoon salt
- 1/2 teaspoon sugar
- 4 slices foie gras, about 1 oz each
- 4 shiitake mushrooms, thinly sliced
- 4 pieces ginkgo nuts, boiled and peeled
- 4 slices carrot, blanched
- 4 snow peas, blanched
- Mitsuba (Japanese parsley) or substitute with cilantro or parsley for garnish
- Soy sauce, for serving

Calories	Servings	Prep Time	Cook Time
150	4	15M	15M

INGREDIENTS:

- 2 cups dashi stock (or substitute with chicken or vegetable broth)
- 4 large eggs
- 1 tablespoon soy sauce
- 1 tablespoon mirin
- 1/2 teaspoon salt
- 1/2 teaspoon sugar
- 4 large shrimp, peeled and deveined
- 4 small scallops
- 4 pieces of crab meat (imitation or real)
- 4 shiitake mushrooms, sliced
- 4 slices of carrot, thinly sliced
- 4 snow peas
- 4 slices kamaboko (fish cake)
- Chopped green onions, for garnish
- Soy sauce, for serving

DIRECTIONS:

1. In a saucepan, bring the dashi stock to a gentle simmer over medium heat.

2. In a mixing bowl, beat the eggs lightly. Add soy sauce, mirin, salt, and sugar. Mix well.

3. Strain the egg mixture through a fine mesh sieve into a large measuring cup or bowl.

4. Prepare four chawanmushi cups or small heatproof bowls. Divide the seafood (shrimp, scallops, crab meat), shiitake mushrooms, carrot slices, snow peas, and kamaboko evenly among the cups.

5. Carefully pour the egg mixture over the seafood and vegetables in each cup, filling them about 80% full.

6. Cover each cup tightly with aluminum foil.

7. Place the cups in a steamer basket or a large pot with a steamer rack. Steam over medium heat for about 15 minutes, or until the chawanmushi is set and no longer jiggles when gently shaken.

8. Once cooked, remove the chawanmushi cups from the steamer and let them cool for a few minutes.

9. Garnish with chopped green onions.

10. Serve the seafood chawanmushi hot, with soy sauce on the side for dipping.

11. Enjoy your delicious Seafood Chawanmushi!

DIRECTIONS:

1. In a saucepan, bring the chicken broth to a gentle simmer over medium heat.

2. In a mixing bowl, beat the eggs lightly. Add soy sauce, mirin, salt, and sugar. Mix well.

3. Strain the egg mixture through a fine mesh sieve into a large measuring cup or bowl.

4. Prepare four chawanmushi cups or small heatproof bowls. Divide the smoked salmon, shiitake mushrooms, snow peas, carrot slices, and kamaboko evenly among the cups.

5. Carefully pour the egg mixture over the ingredients in each cup, filling them about 80% full.

6. Cover each cup tightly with aluminum foil.

7. Place the cups in a steamer basket or a large pot with a steamer rack. Steam over medium heat for about 20 minutes, or until the chawanmushi is set and no longer jiggles when gently shaken.

8. Once cooked, remove the chawanmushi cups from the steamer and let them cool for a few minutes.

9. Garnish with chopped green onions.

10. Serve the smoked salmon chawanmushi hot, with soy sauce on the side for dipping.

11. Enjoy your delicious Smoked Salmon Chawanmushi!

Calories	Servings	Prep Time	Cook Time
180	4	20M	20M

INGREDIENTS:

- 2 cups chicken broth (or dashi stock)
- 4 large eggs
- 1 tablespoon soy sauce
- 1 tablespoon mirin
- 1/2 teaspoon salt
- 1/2 teaspoon sugar
- 4 slices smoked salmon
- 4 shiitake mushrooms, sliced
- 4 snow peas, trimmed
- 4 slices of carrot, thinly sliced
- 4 slices kamaboko (fish cake)
- Chopped green onions, for garnish
- Soy sauce, for serving

Calories	Servings	Prep Time	Cook Time
180	4	15M	20M

Ingredients:

- 2 cups chicken broth (or dashi stock)
- 4 large eggs
- 1 tablespoon soy sauce
- 1 tablespoon mirin
- 1/2 teaspoon salt
- 1/2 teaspoon sugar
- 1/2 cup cooked eel (unagi), cut into bite-sized pieces
- 2 green onions, thinly sliced
- 4 shiitake mushrooms, sliced
- 4 snow peas, trimmed
- 4 slices of carrot, thinly sliced
- 4 slices kamaboko (fish cake)
- Chopped cilantro or parsley, for garnish
- Soy sauce, for serving

Directions:

1. In a saucepan, bring the chicken broth to a gentle simmer over medium heat.
2. In a mixing bowl, beat the eggs lightly. Add soy sauce, mirin, salt, and sugar. Mix well.
3. Strain the egg mixture through a fine mesh sieve into a large measuring cup or bowl.
4. Prepare four chawanmushi cups or small heatproof bowls. Divide the cooked eel and green onions evenly among the cups.
5. Add shiitake mushrooms, snow peas, carrot slices, and kamaboko to each cup.
6. Carefully pour the egg mixture over the ingredients in each cup, filling them about 80% full.
7. Cover each cup tightly with aluminum foil.
8. Place the cups in a steamer basket or a large pot with a steamer rack. Steam over medium heat for about 20 minutes, or until the chawanmushi is set and no longer jiggles when gently shaken.
9. Once cooked, remove the chawanmushi cups from the steamer and let them cool for a few minutes.
10. Garnish with chopped cilantro or parsley.
11. Serve the eel and green onion chawanmushi hot, with soy sauce on the side for dipping.
12. Enjoy your delicious Eel and Green Onion Chawanmushi!

Make it Easy Japanese Home Cooking Cookbook for Beginners:
Simple Recipes for Everyone

ASIN: B0D6LLQV6Y
ASIN: B0D4QFX57B
ASIN: B0D6N6DK3R

Easy Chinese Cookbook for Beginners
Simple Recipes for Authentic Flavors and
Asian Cuisine in English with Pictures

ASIN: B0DCN3LNRR
ASIN: B0DCL5LWVV
ASIN: B0DCPB1QX6

Korean Kimchi Cookbook:
The Essential Guide to Making and
Cooking with Kimchi!

ASIN: B0CQXXM3WT
ASIN: B0CRBJRD13
ASIN: B0C23N9C6K

Easy Korean Cookbook for Beginners:
A Flavorful Journey with Abundant and Simple Recipes Illuminated in Vivid Color

ASIN: B0CPXGHLQ5
ASIN: B0CND5PYMH
ASIN: B0CNJ2DQ8D

Kids Smoothie Recipe Book:
A-Z Guide to Healthy, Yummy, Nutritious Blends They'll Love Making. Illustrated for Kids

ASIN: B0D2JC8J4H
ASIN: B0D2391MWV

Healthy Diabetic Smoothies Cookbook for Beginners:
70 Diabetic-Friendly Colorful Recipe Photos with Glycemic Index (GL), Calorie, and Nutritional Information

ASIN: B0CS3N9C6K
ASIN: B0CR9GMVXT

The Coffee Book:
How to Make the Best Cafe-Style Drinks at Home. Recipes for Your Coffee Machine and More

ASIN: B0D41ZX6H9
ASIN: B0D3SCPVW1
ASIN: B0D4619NSJ

The Anti-Inflammatory Diet:
Your Guide to Reducing Inflammation and Improving Your Health

ASIN: B0CNKRZB56
ASIN: B0CNKKC8MT
ASIN: B0CV2TWM5N

Somatic Psychotherapy Handbook:
Illuminating the Depths of Body-Centered TherapyA Comprehensive Guide

ASIN: B0CZ155HS2
ASIN: B0CYVL3228

||||| ||| ||||| ||||| ||||| ||||| ||||| |||||

1441503вR000046

Made in the USA
Las Vegas, NV
15 December 2024